WITHDRAWN

Religion
In American
History
by Charles C. Haynes

what to teach and how

Association for Supervision and Curriculum Development

ASCD publications present a variety of viewpoints. The views expressed or implied in this publication are not necessarily official positions of the Association.

Printed in the United States of America.
Typeset on Ventura Publisher 2.0.

ISBN: 0-87120-166-6
Stock No.: 611-90084
Price: $16.95

Library of Congress Cataloging in Publication Data

Haynes, Charles C.
  Religion in American history: what to teach and how / Charles C. Haynes.
      p.   cm.
   ISBN 0-87120-166-6
   1. United States—Religion—Study and teaching (Secondary)—United States.
I. Title.
BL2525.H39   1990
291'.071'273—dc20

90-33535
CIP

Contents

About the Author

Charles C. Haynes is Project Director for the Americans United Research Foundation. He also currently serves as president of the National Council on Religion and Public Education and as chairperson of the Religion in Schools Committee of the National Council for the Social Studies. His first book, *Religious Freedom in America: A Teacher's Guide*, has been distributed to 30,000 teachers nationwide. Haynes is also one of the authors of *Living With Our Deepest Differences: Religious Liberty in a Pluralistic Society*, a new social studies curriculum developed by the Williamsburg Charter Foundation.

Haynes holds a master's degree in religion and education from Harvard Divinity School and a Ph.D. in theological studies from Emory University. He formerly taught world religions at Randolph-Macon College and social studies in both public and private secondary schools.

Acknowledgments

This book is a collaborative effort. Part I is based on the work of Timothy Smith, professor of history at the Johns Hopkins University. I am very grateful to him and to the ASCD panel that helped to revise and expand Professor Smith's original list: Diane Berreth, Edwin Gaustad, Herbert Greenhut, and Sister Mary Jessica Karlinger.

Part II owes much to the advice and encouragement of the talented people in the Education Branch of the National Archives, particularly Branch Chief Elsie Freeman and education specialists Wynell Burroughs Schamel and Jean Mueller. A special word of thanks to Wynell Schamel for her substantial contributions to the form and content of the document section. I am indebted to Edwin Gaustad and Sister Mary Jessica Karlinger for their careful reading of the manuscript. Sister Mary Jessica also suggested two of the documents.

The Americans United Research Foundation, under the leadership of Executive Director Robert L. Maddox, supported the development of this book. Regina Hayden, project assistant at the Foundation, contributed in many important ways to the completion of the project.

Finally, I wish to acknowledge with gratitude how much I have learned from the outstanding social studies teachers who have worked with me in the institutes and workshops during the past four years.

CHARLES C. HAYNES

Foreword

Religion in American History is a unique ASCD publication. It comes to us at a time when American classroom teachers, desirous of filling in some obvious gaps in history textbooks, are searching for ways to teach about the influence of religion and religious events in American history. The book grew from author Charles Haynes' participation on an ASCD panel that identified and examined those influences and recommended 29 areas for inclusion in the enriched study of social studies and American literature.

The heart of the book is Haynes' own recommendations for using primary source documents to teach about historical events that were rooted in religious beliefs and practices. Taking into account the already-crowded curriculum, Haynes explains how teachers can use documents simultaneously to address several important academic objectives. He urges teachers to copy and use the 13 facsimiles in the book and the background information that accompanies each one to help students interpret history based on their own reading of the documents. Suggested discussion questions, research topics, and additional resources allow teachers to expand lessons in a variety of ways.

I urge school boards and teachers alike to pay particular attention to Part 3 of the book, in which Haynes answers some common questions about the role of religion in the classroom. The primary source documents alone show us that religion has played an important role in our nation's history and should not be ignored in the classroom. Today's technology will undoubtedly make many more documents readily available to students and educators, placing the actual artifacts of history at their fingertips. Haynes provides a valuable service in structuring the meaningful use of such documents.

PATRICIA C. CONRAN
ASCD President, 1989-1990

Introduction

One of the most significant developments in American education today is the growing recognition that study about religion ought to be included in all areas of the curriculum. Throughout the country, from California to North Carolina, school districts are issuing new guidelines that mandate more discussion of religion in the classroom, particularly in the study of United States and world history.

The movement to include more about religion in the public school curriculum springs from major changes in America's educational and political climate. Although the reasons for these changes are many, three factors stand out as having special significance for the public schools:

• In the mid-1980s textbook studies, coupled with the "textbook trials" in Tennessee and Alabama, alerted educators to the serious neglect of religion in most public school textbooks. This neglect was due, in part at least, to fear of controversy and to widespread misunderstanding of the Supreme Court rulings of the early 1960s declaring state-sponsored religious practices in public schools to be unconstitutional. What many educators did not understand (or chose to ignore) was that in those same rulings, the Court clearly indicated that teaching *about* religion was not only constitutional, but necessary for a good education. Recent reports, notably one issued by the Association for Supervision and Curriculum Development, have attempted to end the confusion by discussing the importance of study about religion for understanding history and culture.

• In 1988, The Williamsburg Charter, a reaffirmation of the Religious Liberty clauses of the First Amendment, was signed by religious, political, and educational leaders representing the broad spectrum of American society. The Charter serves to remind Americans of how vitally important it is for citizens of all faiths or none to understand and appreciate the principles of religious liberty and the proper role of religion in public life. To help teachers convey these principles in the classroom, The Williamsburg Charter Foundation has developed a new curriculum, "Living With Our Deepest Differences: Religious Liberty in a Pluralistic Society," that contains lessons for use in elementary and secondary social studies courses.

• A coalition of sixteen national religious and educational organizations published "Religion in the Public School Curriculum: Questions and Answers" in 1988, outlining the proper role of religion in the public school classroom. A similar coalition produced "Religious Holidays in the Public Schools: Questions and Answers" in 1989. These historic agreements offer powerful support for school boards, administrators, and teachers as they work to encourage study about religion in ways that are constitutionally permissible and educationally sound.

The new consensus supporting teaching about religion and religious liberty comes at a critical time for public education. Expanding pluralism in the United States confronts our schools with unprecedented challenges. America has shifted from the largely Protestant pluralism of the 18th century to a pluralism that now includes people of all faiths and a growing number of people who indicate no religious preference. New populations of Muslims, Buddhists, and many other religious and ethnic groups are entering schools throughout the nation. If we are to continue to live together as one nation of many faiths, it is a matter of some urgency that students develop a strong commitment to the First Amendment principles of religious liberty and a clear understanding of the role religion plays in history and society.

Now that there is a significant national trend to teach more about religion and religious liberty, the question for social studies teachers is no longer "Should I teach about religion?" but rather, "What should I teach, and how should I do it?" This book begins to answer these questions by focusing on a good starting point for social studies professionals: teaching the role of religion and the significance of religious liberty in American history. The best approach, and the one adopted in this book, is the *natural inclusion* of religion where appropriate in the history courses now being taught.

Part I of this book provides a comprehensive list of the significant religious influences in the story of our nation. Much of what is listed is directly related to themes already discussed in most high school history classes. Teachers need not, therefore, teach a different course. The same course may be taught, but with a different emphasis at those points where religious movements and influences are crucial to understanding the events of history.

Part II describes a practical method for natural inclusion of religious influences using original source documents. Documents provide an immediate encounter with history, giving students a hands-on experience with the materials of the historian. The sample documents included here are meant to suggest the wide variety of document facsimiles available for classroom use.

At the end of the book, in Part III, teachers will find consensus statements and general guidelines for teaching about religion in a public school setting. The key distinction made in all of the statements is the difference between teaching religion, which is unconstitutional, and teaching *about* religion, which is an important part of a complete education. Teachers are reminded that teaching about religious influences in American history must not be taken as an opportunity to either promote or denigrate religion. Religious issues in history should be discussed with the same balance and sensitivity that teachers are required to bring to all historical events and ideas.

Having worked closely with hundreds of social studies teachers throughout the nation for the past five years, I am convinced that the social studies profession is fully capable of handling a more comprehensive discussion of religion in history. Given proper materials and adequate support, most teachers do an excellent job with issues that are sometimes complex and often controversial.

Too few Americans appreciate the crucial role of the social studies teacher in shaping the destiny of our nation. We must not forget that it is primarily in the civics, history, and government classrooms of our schools that young people learn what it is to be responsible citizens.

Fortunately, the United States has many enthusiastic, highly motivated teachers of history and citizenship who convey the excitement of history and the genius of the American experiment in freedom. These teachers tell me that they are ready and willing to enrich their courses with more discussion of religion and religious liberty. All they ask is to be provided with good materials to help them do the job. This book is dedicated, then, to the frontline guardians of America's future, the social studies teachers of the United States.

CHARLES C. HAYNES

PART

I

Religious Influences in American History

A Curriculum Guide

Many significant developments in American history have turned on religious events and movements secondary schools should include in their history curriculums. Most educators agree that without proper attention to the role of religion, the story of America is incomplete and distorted.

In view of the growing recognition that including religion and religious liberty in the curriculum is necessary and important, teachers of American history need to know what is being asked of them: what is now left out of the curriculum and what ought to be included. Responding to this need, Timothy Smith, professor of history at the Johns Hopkins University, developed a list of significant religious influences in the history of the United States. An ASCD panel, working with Dr. Smith, revised and expanded the list for publication in this book. The members of the panel were:

Diane Berreth, Director of Field Services, Association of Supervision and Curriculum Development, Alexandria, Va.

Edwin Gaustad, Professor of History, University of California, Riverside

Herbert Greenhut, Social Studies Teacher, Wagner Junior High School, New York City, N.Y.

Charles C. Haynes, Project Director, Americans United Research Foundation, Silver Spring, Md.

Sister Mary Jessica Karlinger, Social Studies Teacher, Notre Dame Academy, Middleburg, Virginia

Timothy Smith, Professor of History, Johns Hopkins University, Baltimore, Md.

The panel offers the following list of 29 religious influences in American history as a general guide for teachers of social studies and literature who are seeking to enrich their courses with appropriate consideration of the role religions have played in history and society. Also included are recommended readings for each area of study.

1. Religious motivations in Spanish, English, and French exploration and colonization. These movements can be understood properly only in the context of the Renaissance and Reformation.

☐ Quinn, David B., ed. (1979). *New American World*. 5 vols. New York: Arno Press and Hector Bye, Inc.

☐ Wright, Louis B. (1970). *Gold, Glory, and the Gospel*. New York: Atheneum Press.

2. The existence of Native American religions and civilization prior to and during European settlement. Knowledge of the content of Native American religions during the early period is limited, being largely derived from Christian missionary accounts. This bias, however, can be corrected by more recent anthropological studies, including those of current tribal religions.

☐ Beck, Peggy V., and Anna L. Walters. (1977). *The Sacred: Ways of Knowledge, Sources of Life*. Isaile, Arizona: Navajo Community College Press.

☐ Neihardt, John. (1979). *Black Elk Speaks: Being the Life Story of a Holy Man of the Oglala Sioux*. Lincoln: University of Nebraska Press.

☐ Underhill, Ruth M. (1972). *Red Man's Religion: Beliefs and Practices of the Indians North of Mexico*. Chicago: University of Chicago Press.

3. The role of Spanish missions as social institutions in the first Spanish settlements and in expanding the Hispanic frontier northward, 1550–1848, in what is now the southwestern and western United States.

☐ Ellis, J. T. (1965). *Catholics in Colonial America*. Baltimore: Helicon Press.

☐ Gibson, Charles. (1967). *Spain in America*. New American Nation Series. New York: Harper & Row.

4. The role of Puritan religion in the foundation of the Bible Commonwealths of New England and in the shaping of the later nation's sense of mission. The Puritans were convinced that they had been led by God to create a "New Israel" based on biblical law that would be a model for old England. Though they wanted freedom for their own faith, they did not believe in or wish to establish freedom of religion for others, as witnessed by their attitude toward Quakers and Baptists.

☐ Morgan, Edmund S. (1962). *The Puritan Dilemma: The Story of John Winthrop*. Boston: Little, Brown.

☐ Stout, Harry S. (1986). *The New England Soul: Preaching and Religious Culture in Colonial New England*. New York: Oxford University Press.

5. The development of religious pluralism in the colonies of Rhode Island, New York, New Jersey, Pennsylvania, Maryland, and to a large degree, in the Southern colonies. Long before the American Revolution, there was increasing public acceptance of the separation of church and state, especially in Rhode Island and Pennsylvania. Early pluralism was chiefly Protestant, of course. It involved a number of nationalities (Dutch, English, German, and African) and a host of religious denominations, from the formerly established churches to the radically pacifist Quaker and Mennonite communities.

- ☐ Balmer, Randall. (1989). *A Perfect Babel of Confusion: Dutch Religion and English Culture in the Middle Colonies*. New York: Oxford University Press.

- ☐ Bonomi, Patricia U. (1986). *Under the Cope of Heaven: Religion, Society, and Politics in Colonial America*. New York: Oxford University Press.

- ☐ Morgan, Edmund S. (1987). *Roger Williams: The Church and the State*. New York: W.W. Norton.

6. The work of Indian missions in shaping the relationships of the colonists with Native Americans, from John Eliot in New England through the Quakers, peace churches, and Methodists to Roman Catholic missions on the northern plains and in Alaska after the Civil War.

- ☐ Beaver, R. P. (1966). *Church, State, and the American Indians*. St. Louis: Concordia Publishing House.

- ☐ Bowden, Henry W. (1981). *American Indians and Christian Missions: Studies in Cultural Conflict*. Chicago History of American Religion Series. Chicago: University of Chicago Press.

7. The influence of the great colonial revivals, often called "The Great Awakening," 1728–1790, in the making of an independent republic and in the realignment of the denominations.

- ☐ Heimert, Alan, and Perry Miller, eds. (1967). *The Great Awakening: Documents Illustrating the Crisis and Its Consequences*. Indianapolis: Bobbs-Merrill.

- ☐ Isaac, Rhys. (1982). *The Transformation of Virginia, 1740–1790*. Institute of Early American History and Culture Series. Chapel Hill: University of North Carolina Press.

8. The contribution of the Enlightenment's ideals of religious liberty and "civic virtue" to the thinking of the Founding Fathers, especially Thomas Jefferson, James Madison, and George Mason. Popular support for a Bill of Rights, containing the provision that "Congress shall make no law respecting an establishment of religion, or prohibiting the free exercise thereof," came from many organized religious groups.

- ☐ Gaustad, Edwin S. (1987). *Faith of Our Fathers: Religion and the New Nation*. San Francisco: Harper & Row.

- ☐ May, Henry F. (1976). *The Enlightenment in America*. New York: Oxford University Press.

- ☐ Miller, William. (1987). *The First Liberty: Religion and the American Republic*. New York: Alfred A. Knopf.

9. The growth of the anti-Catholic and anti-foreign nativist movement in the first half of the 19th century, culminating in the 1840s and 1850s in the Know-Nothing party. A resurgence of similar sentiments in the late 19th century contributed to anti-Semitism, opposition to immigration, and the rise of the Ku Klux Klan.

- ☐ Belth, Nathan C. (1979). *A Promise to Keep: A Narrative of the American Encounter with Anti-Semitism*. New York: Times Books.

- ☐ Billington, Ray A. (1938). *The Protestant Crusade, 1800–1860: A Study of the Origins of American Nativism*. New York: Macmillan.

- ☐ Higham, John. (1963). *Strangers in the Land: Patterns of American Nativism, 1860–1925*. New York: Atheneum Press.

10. The place of religiously inspired moralism, Protestant millennialism, Methodist perfectionism, and the Christian Utopianism (exhibited by such groups as the Shakers) in 19th century movements for social reform.

- ☐ Foster, Lawrence. (1981). *Religion and Sexuality: Three American Communal Experiments in the Nineteenth Century*. New York: Oxford University Press.

- ☐ Gaustad, Edwin S., ed. (1974). *Rise of Adventism: Religion and Society in Mid-Nineteenth-Century America*. New York: Harper & Row.

11. The role of Protestantism in the founding of American colleges and in the shaping of the common school movement. The latter preceded the public school movement and generally merged with it. On a mobile frontier, no one congregation was strong enough to support schools for

even its own children, much less for all. By 1830, however, most churches and synagogues had discovered their common agreement about moral values, though Catholics and Jews objected to the Protestant orientation of public schooling. Catholics continued to develop their own parish and private schools.

- ☐ Cremin, Lawrence A. (1972). *American Education: The Colonial Experience, 1607–1783.* New York: Harper & Row.

- ☐ Cremin, Lawrence A. (1980). *American Education: The National Experience, 1783–1896.* New York: Harper & Row.

- ☐ Warch, Richard. (1973). *School of the Prophets: Yale College, 1701–1740.* New Haven: Yale University Press.

12. The part played by religion, as practiced by both whites and blacks, in the movement to abolish slavery, 1825–1866. The success of the abolitionist movement, however, should not obscure southern appeals during the same period to scriptural precedents to defend slavery.

- ☐ Smith, H. Shelton. (1972). *In His Image, But . . . : Racism in Southern Religion, 1780–1910.* Durham: Duke University Press.

- ☐ Thomas, Benjamin. (1950). *P. Theodore Weld: Crusader for Freedom.* New Brunswick: Rutgers University Press.

13. The function of religion, Catholic and Jewish as well as Protestant, in the formation of new communities on the frontier—as seen especially in the settlements of western New York, the Shenandoah and Mississippi valleys, Utah, and the Great Northwest Territory—and religion's place in the emergence of a mixed English and Hispanic culture in the Southwest.

- ☐ Dolan, Jay P. (1978). *Catholic Revivalism: The American Experience, 1830–1900.* Notre Dame: University of Notre Dame Press.

- ☐ Johnson, Charles A. (1955; 1985 reprint). *The Frontier Camp Meeting: Religion's Harvest Time.* Dallas: Southern Methodist University Press.

14. The significance of the great revivals of religion led by Charles G. Finney, Dwight L. Moody, and the Catholic Redemptorist fathers, 1810–1890. The rise of large voluntary associations such as the American Bible Society, the American Sunday School Union, and the American Temperance Society is part of this movement. Urban social work, schooling for poor children, and freedom for African Americans were partly fruits of the moral quickening of religious awakenings. At the end

of the century, American Jewish women emerged as leaders of similar social crusades; their views were anchored in the same biblical texts that Protestant and Roman Catholic reformers had long employed.

- ☐ Foster, C. I. (1960). *An Errand of Mercy: The United Evangelical Front.* Chapel Hill: University of North Carolina Press.

- ☐ McLoughlin, William. (1959). *Modern Revivalism.* New York: Ronald Press Co.

- ☐ Smith, Timothy L. (1957). *Revivalism and Social Reform in Mid-Nineteenth Century America.* Nashville, Tenn.: Abingdon Press.

15. The rise of indigenous religious movements in 19th century America, such as the Latter-day Saints (Mormons), Disciples and churches of Christ, Seventh-Day Adventists, Christian Scientists, and Jehovah's Witnesses.

- ☐ Arrington, Leonard J., and Davis Bitton. (1979). *The Mormon Experience: A History of the Latter-day Saints.* New York: Alfred A. Knopf.

- ☐ Moore, R. Laurence. (1986). *Religious Outsiders and the Making of Americans.* New York: Oxford University Press.

16. The centrality of religion in African American culture after the Civil War and the implications of this religious tradition for the history of African American schooling. Without knowing these implications, neither white nor black students can understand the situation of modern politics, where Martin Luther King, Jr., Jesse Jackson, and other ministers have led important movements centered in the African American churches.

- ☐ Hill, Samuel S., ed. (1983). *Religion in the Southern States.* Macon: Mercer University Press.

- ☐ Sernett, Milton C., ed. (1985). *Afro-American Religious History: A Documentary Witness.* Durham: Duke University Press.

17. The place of the Bible in American literature and law. Biblical language was an important element in 19th century literature as well as in American court decisions.

- ☐ Frye, Northrop. (1983). *The Great Code: The Bible and Literature.* New York: Harcourt, Brace, Jovanovich.

- ☐ Gaustad, Edwin, and Walter Harrelson, general eds. *The Bible in American Culture Series.* 6 vols. Philadelphia, Pa., and Decatur, Ga.: Fortress Press and Scholars Press.

18. The place of overseas missions, Catholic as well as Protestant, in American foreign relations, from the first expressions of national interest in the Near East in the 1830s to such events as the Boxer Rebellion in China, the Spanish-American War, and the modern involvement of black and white Americans in shaping our nation's policies toward Africa and Latin America.

- ☐ Considine, Robert B. (1950). *The Maryknoll Story.* New York: Doubleday and Co.

- ☐ Hutchison, William R. (1987). *Errand to the World: American Protestant Thought & Foreign Missions.* Chicago: University of Chicago Press.

- ☐ Latourette, Kenneth Scott. (1958). *Christianity in a Revolutionary Age.* 5 vols. New York: Harper & Row.

19. Moral and religious consensus in the Progressive Era. Examples include the Women's Christian Temperance Movement, which eventually triumphed in the adoption of the Eighteenth Amendment forbidding alcoholic beverages; the labor union movement, as represented in the leadership of the International Ladies Garment Workers Union by New York Jews; the movement for municipal reform; reaction to the Triangle Shirt Factory fire; the struggle to temper the excesses of unbridled capitalism; and idealistic attitudes toward World War I, continued in the pacifist movement of the 1920s. Students cannot understand Woodrow Wilson's policies in either domestic or foreign affairs without knowledge of these developments.

- ☐ Abell, Aaron I., ed. (1968). *American Catholic Thought on Social Questions.* Indianapolis: Bobbs-Merrill.

- ☐ Hopkins, C. Howard. (1940; 1967 reprint). *The Rise of the Social Gospel in American Protestantism, 1865–1895.* New Haven: Yale University Press.

20. The centrality of religion in the new immigrant subcultures formed in America between 1880 and 1910, including Czech Roman Catholic, Ukrainian Greek Catholic, Romanian Orthodox, Hungarian and Finnish Protestant, and Asian Buddhist (especially in Hawaii). Many Jewish subcommunities existed, including the one that was chiefly German, called "Reform," and the one designated "Orthodox," composed of Polish, Russian, Romanian and other Jews from central and eastern Europe. Each community was built around religious congregations; each helped its members adjust to life in the United States. In many Catholic communities, this purpose was also served by the local parish school.

☐ Dolan, Jay P. (1983). *The Immigrant Church: New York's Irish and German Catholics, 1815–1865.* Indiana: University of Notre Dame Press.

☐ Handlin, Oscar. (1951). *The Uprooted: The Epic Story of the Great Migrations that Made the American People.* Boston: Little, Brown.

☐ Howe, Irving. (1976). *World of Our Fathers.* New York: Harcourt, Brace, Jovanovich.

21. The role of religion in providing health care to the urban poor in the 19th century, including the Lutheran, Methodist, and Baptist deaconess movements; Roman Catholic sisterhoods; Seventh-Day Adventist sanatoriums; and Jewish hospitals.

☐ Marty, Martin E., and Kenneth L. Vaux, eds. (1982). *Health/ Medicine and the Faith Traditions: An Inquiry into Religion and Medicine.* Philadelphia: Fortress Press. Traditions include Jewish, Catholic, Islamic, Reformed, and others. Available from Books on Demand, phone 800-521-0600.

☐ Numbers, R. L., and D. W. Amundsen, eds. (1986). *Caring and Curing: Historical Essays on Health, Medicine, and the Faith Traditions.* New York: Macmillan.

22. The significance of the rise of Fundamentalists to the restructuring of evangelical movements in the 20th century. The distinctions between Fundamentalists and the more traditional evangelicals (Southern Presbyterians, Southern Baptists, Disciples and churches of Christ, and Wesleyans) are important. The Fundamentalists deeply affect conservative American politics to this very day. Students need to understand the tremendous growth of the Pentecostals and Roman Catholic charismatics and of such conservative denominations as the Missouri Synod of Lutherans or the Christian Reformed. They should also know how the resurgence of evangelicalism affected the peace churches and the African American denominations.

☐ Hutchison, William R. (1976). *The Modernist Impulse in American Protestantism.* Cambridge: Harvard University Press.

☐ Marsden, George. (1980). *Fundamentalism and American Culture: The Shaping of Twentieth-Century Evangelicalism, 1870–1925.* New York: Oxford University Press.

23. The place of religion in the civil rights crusade surrounding Martin Luther King, Jr., and especially the roles of American Protestant, Jewish, and Catholic clergy in it. The moral and religious basis of King's

commitment to civil rights was deeply rooted in his experience as an evangelical Baptist clergyman. The moral outrage of Jewish rabbis, who had during the previous 30 years of the New Deal considered themselves allies of African Americans, was echoed in the large commitment of Protestant and Roman Catholic laity and clergy to the civil rights movement. Nevertheless, the opposition of many religious congregations to civil rights, then and now, should be noted.

- ☐ King, Martin Luther. (1958). *Stride Toward Freedom.* New York: Harper & Row.

- ☐ Oates, Stephen B. (1982). *Let the Trumpet Sound: The Life of Martin Luther King, Jr. New York: Harper & Row.*

- ☐ Wilmore, Gayraud S., and James H. Cone, eds. (1979). *Black Theology: A Documentary History, 1966–1979.* Maryknoll: Orbis Books.

24. The work of Reinhold Niebuhr and the "political realists," before and during World War II, in opposing the pacifism and isolation that had penetrated American religious communities. Isolationism, Niebuhr and his many students and followers believed, weakened the nation's resolve to oppose Nazism. Nevertheless, leaders of the Christian churches and of the American government did not translate this opposition into measures aimed at saving Jews from concentration camps.

- ☐ Fox, Richard. (1986). *Reinhold Niebuhr: A Biography.* New York: Pantheon Books.

- ☐ Kegley, C. W., ed. (1984). *Reinhold Niebuhr: His Religious, Social, and Political Thought.* Rev. ed. New York: Pilgrim Press.

- ☐ Niebuhr, Reinhold. (1932). *Moral Man and Immoral Society: A Study in Ethics and Politics.* New York: Scribner.

25. The recent revival of the religiously based peace movement, based on a convergence of religious forces from all faiths. The Catholic bishops have come to the verge of condemning all nuclear war, including the threat of massive retaliation to deter it. The Mormon bishops have spoken out to prevent the use of Utah land as a base for movable MX missiles. The Methodist bishops have joined religious liberals in the Unitarian and Quaker churches to oppose such weapons. And the evangelical New Call to Peacemaking, uniting evangelical Mennonites, Brethren (Dunkers), and Friends, has led the peace crusade among Protestants.

☐ Brock, Peter. (1968). *Pacifism in the United States: From the Colonial Era to the First World War.* Princeton: Princeton University Press.

☐ Sider, Ronald J., and Richard Taylor. (1983). *Nuclear Holocaust and Christian Hope: A Book for Christian Peacemakers.* New York: Paulist Press.

26. The revitalization of Judaism continues. Adolph Hitler's early anti-Semitism intensified a flight to this country of small groups of Jews from central and eastern European communities. Within this country, publicly expressed anti-Semitism evoked a counterwave of visible Jewish self-affirmation. Reform, Conservative, Orthodox, and Reconstructionist Jews have reasserted their Jewish identity in bold new ways, and Reform Judaism has been particularly visible in the advocacy of social justice.

☐ Philipson, David. (1967). *The Reform Movement in Judaism.* New York: KTAV Publishing House.

☐ Poll, Solomon. (1962). *The Hasidic Community of Williamsburg.* New York: Free Press of Glencoe.

☐ Potok, Chaim. (1969). *The Promise.* New York: Alfred A. Knopf.

☐ Ruderman, Jerome. (1974). *Jews in American History: A Teacher's Guide.* New York: The Anti-Defamation League of B'nai B'rith.

☐ Waxman, Mordecai, ed. (1958, 1970 reprint). *Tradition and Change: The Development of Conservative Judaism.* New York: Burning Bush Press.

27. Developments within the Roman Catholic faith, especially since the Second Vatican Council, such as the spread of a biblical approach to piety, liturgical renewal, ecumenical involvement, and the charismatic movement. Public discussion and debate within the American Catholic community about such matters as the role of authority, peace and justice issues, contraception and abortion, and the role of women have also become more evident. As Catholics have struggled with the question of how to be authentically Catholic in an American context, they have also gained greater acceptance as participants in American public life, as evidenced, for example, by the election of John F. Kennedy to the presidency.

☐ Dolan, Jay P. (1987). *The American Catholic Experience: A History from Colonial Times to the Present.* New York: Doubleday.

☐ Flannery, Austin, ed. (1975). *Vatican Council II: The Conciliar and Post Conciliar Documents.* Vol. I. Northport, N.Y.: Costello.

☐ Hennessey, James. (1979). *American Catholics: A History of the Roman Catholic Community in the United States.* New York: Oxford University Press.

☐ Kelly, George A. (1981). *The Battle for the American Church.* New York: Doubleday, Image Books.

28. The involvement of American religious communities in international controversies, such as apartheid in South Africa and the many conflicts in Central America and the Middle East.

☐ Geyer, Alan F. (1963). *Piety and Politics: American Protestantism in the World Arena.* Richmond, Va.: John Knox.

☐ Gordis, Robert. (1962). *The Root and the Branch: Judaism and the Free Society.* Chicago: The University of Chicago.

☐ Hanna, Mary T. (1979). *Catholics and American Politics.* Cambridge, Mass.: Harvard University.

☐ Nichols, J. Bruce. (1988). *The Uneasy Alliance: Religion, Refugee Work, and U.S. Foreign Policy.* New York: Oxford University Press.

29. Expanding religious pluralism in the United States, as revealed in the expansion of the numbers of American Muslims and Buddhists, and in the rise of new religious movements. Since 1776 religious sects and denominations in the United States have grown from several dozen to several thousand. The new challenges of living together in a pluralistic society are evident in the increasing numbers of church-state cases heard by the U.S. Supreme Court and in the many controversies concerning the proper role of religion in the public schools.

☐ Miller, Robert T., and Ronald B. Flowers. (1987). *Toward Benevolent Neutrality: Church, State, and the Supreme Court.* 3rd ed. Waco, Texas: Baylor University Press.

☐ Littell, Franklin H., ed. (1978). *Religious Liberty in the Crossfire of Creeds.* Philadelphia: Ecumenical Press.

☐ Needleman, Jacob. (1970). *The New Religions.* New York: Doubleday.

☐ Wuthnow, Robert. (1988). *The Restructuring of American Religion.* Princeton: Princeton University Press.

Recommended General Works

Ahlstrom, Sydney E. (1972). *A Religious History of the American People*
New Haven: Yale University Press.

Gaustad, Edwin S., ed. (1982, 1983). *A Documentary History of Religion
in America.* 2 vols. Grand Rapids, Mich.: William B. Eerdmans.

Haynes, Charles C. (1986). *Religious Freedom in America: A Teacher's
Guide.* Silver Spring: Americans United Research Foundation.

Hudson, Winthrop S. (1987). *Religion in America: An Historical Account
of the Development of American Religious Life.* 4th ed. New York:
Macmillan.

Lippy, Charles H., and Peter W. Williams, eds. (1988). *Encyclopedia of
American Religious Experience.* 3 vols. New York: Scribner.

Marty, Martin E. (1984). *Pilgrims in Their Own Land: Five Hundred Years
of Religion in America.* Boston: Little, Brown.

Spivey, R., E. Gaustad, and R. Allen, eds. (1989). *Pathways to Pluralism.*
Menlo Park, Calif.: Addison-Wesley.

Wilson, John F., and Donald L. Drakeman, eds. (1987). *Church and State
in American History.* Boston: Beacon Press.

Additional Resources

The Williamsburg Charter Foundation has developed a new curriculum, "Living with Our Deepest Differences: Religious Liberty in a Pluralistic Society." It contains lessons for upper elementary, middle school, and high school students on the history and significance of the First Amendment Religious Liberty clauses and their decisive contribution to individual and communal liberty and to American democracy. For more information, contact the Foundation at (202) 857-2360.

Resources for teaching about religion are available through the Distribution Center of the National Council on Religion and Public Education (N162 Lagomarcino Hall, Iowa State University, Ames, Iowa 50011). NCRPE provides curriculum guides and sample lessons in several subject areas. The NCRPE journal, *Religion and Public Education*, is a clearinghouse for information about religion studies in public education and other issues concerning religion and the schools.

PART
II

Using Documents to Teach About Religion

An Effective Teaching Method

One of the most effective and accessible ways to integrate study about religions into the curriculum is to use primary source documents. The approach outlined here has been developed in collaboration with Wynell Burroughs Schamel, education specialist at the National Archives, and in workshops with teachers throughout the country.

The documents in this book are only a few samples of the wide variety of primary source materials concerning religion that are available for classroom use. I encourage teachers to build an extensive set of documents as a resource for teaching about religious influences in all periods of American history and literature.

Why Use Documents?

The widespread demand to include religion in the curriculum puts already burdened teachers in a difficult position. Inadequate textbook treatment of religion, the dearth of good supplementary materials, and the already crowded curriculum prevent teachers from adding much about the role of religion to existing courses.

Teaching with documents effectively overcomes some of the barriers to teaching about religion in at least four concrete ways:

1. Primary source documents concerning religion are readily available, educationally sound supplements to textbooks.

2. Used creatively, documents introduce the religious dimension of history and society without adding significantly to the amount of material that must be covered in a given course. Consider the congressional resolution condemning General Grant's order expelling the Jews (document 7). This document might be used to teach subject matter already taught in many social studies classrooms—economic problems during the Civil War, the relationship between Congress and the military, suspension of civil rights during wartime—and, at the same time, involve students in a discussion of anti-Semitism, the Religious Liberty clauses of the First Amendment, the history of Jews in the United States, and related religious liberty themes. Using such a document allows the teacher to achieve several important academic objectives simultaneously.

3. A single document can not only address a number of subjects, it can also be easily inserted into a variety of places in the curriculum. This flexibility is illustrated by the documents selected for this book. The anti-Catholic memorial presented to Congress (document 6), for

17

example, might be used when teaching about Article VI of the Constitution, nativism, immigration, the campaigns of Al Smith and John Kennedy, or other topics in history and government. Again, teaching with documents supports the presentation of required material and allows consideration of related religious elements in our history and society.

4. Discussing the role of religion in history and literature may raise controversial and emotional issues. When controversy does arise, teachers have found documents to be a practical and objective way to focus the discussion. Examining documents from history helps students move beyond gut reactions and prejudices and discover first-hand the roots of religious events and conflicts.

Perhaps the most compelling reason for using documents, however, is that documents are written by people who actually witnessed or participated in an event. Using these sources can make the events of history personal and immediate. The teacher can create a laboratory in the classroom, giving students direct access to the tools of the historian or writer and encouraging students to analyze and evaluate for themselves the building blocks of history. Documents push students to raise further questions and seek more information. Critical thinking skills are inevitably strengthened as students learn to recognize points of view, biases, contradictions, and limitations in the documents examined. Students quickly learn that just as there is more than one valid interpretation of primary source materials, there is more than one way to understand history.

Guidelines for Using Documents

Since primary source documents are unfamiliar to most students, working with them in the classroom requires some teacher preparation. First and foremost, the teacher must establish the context for the document. Each document in this book is accompanied by a "historical background" section written primarily for the teacher. In some cases, the teacher may wish to distribute copies of this section to students for background reading. Without adequate understanding of the historical setting and societal conditions, documents can easily mislead and confuse students. The dangers of misunderstanding are especially acute when religion is being discussed.

We highly recommend that students work directly with the document and not with a transcription. (All of the documents included in this collection may be reproduced freely.) Although the age and legibility of many documents demand some struggle to decipher the wording of the record, working directly with the document allows students to examine the raw material of history in the way a historian might.

Given the proper context and some assistance, students can be motivated by documents to explore the personal side of history—the emotions, values, and attitudes of the people whose lives were touched by the events being examined. The excerpts from Molly Goodrich's journal (document 5) and the letter from an African American minister (document 9) vividly illustrate how an abstract discussion of religious persecution or Reconstruction can be made immediate and real in the classroom.

Because many documents are incomplete, students raise questions that are not answered in the document itself. These questions provide natural opportunities for the teacher to encourage further exploration through reading and research. Each document in this book is accompanied by suggested activities and research topics and a list of classroom resources.

Where to Find Documents

Primary source documents related to the role of religion in American history are available in archives, libraries, historical society collections, and personal records. The National Archives has branches throughout the country that provide access to the records of the federal government. Many states have historical societies and libraries with extensive document collections. The Massachusetts Historical Society, for example, has a number of Roger Williams' letters in its Winthrop collection. The Virginia State Library, like many state libraries and archives, publishes a set of facsimiles that includes several religious freedom documents.

The National Archives has developed a series of excellent document-based teaching units about various periods of United States history. Each unit contains many facsimiles of primary source documents for use in the classroom and a comprehensive teacher's guide. The units on the U.S. Constitution and the Bill of Rights contain a number of documents related to religion and religious liberty in American history. These materials are available from Social Issues Resources Services, Inc. (SIRS), P.O. Box 2507, Boca Raton, Florida 33427.

I will help teachers locate documents for teaching about religions and religious freedom. The education specialists at the National Archives can also offer advice about the use of documents. Feel free to write or call us at these locations:

Charles C. Haynes
Project Director
Americans United Research
  Foundation
900 Silver Spring Ave.
Silver Spring, MD 20910
301/588-2382

Wynell Schamel
Education Specialist
Education Branch, NEE
National Archives
Washington, D.C. 20408
202/724-0455

At the Americans United Research Foundation, we offer an annual summer institute for social studies teachers that focuses on the history of religious freedom in America. The National Archives holds an annual workshop for teachers on the use of primary sources in the classroom. It also has 11 field branches:

ATLANTA
The National Archives
1557 St. Joseph Avenue
East Point, GA 30344
404/246-7477

BOSTON
The National Archives
380 Trapelo Road
Waltham, MA 02154
617/647-8100

CHICAGO
The National Archives
7358 South Pulaski Road
Chicago, IL 60629
312/581-7816

DENVER
The National Archives
P.O. Box 25307
Denver, CO 80225
303/236-0817

FORT WORTH
The National Archives
P.O. Box 6216
Fort Worth, TX 76115
817/334-5525

KANSAS CITY
The National Archives
2312 East Bannister Road
Kansas City, MO 64131
816/926-6934

LOS ANGELES
The National Archives
2400 Avila Road, 1st Floor
Laguna Niguel, CA 92677-6719
714/643-4241

NEW YORK
The National Archives
Bldg. 22, Mil. Ocean Terrace
Bayonne, NJ 07002-5388
201/823-7252

PHILADELPHIA
The National Archives
9th & Market Streets, Room 1350
Philadelphia, PA 19107
215/597-3000

SEATTLE
The National Archives
6125 Sand Point Way, N.E.
Seattle, WA 98115
206/526-6507

SAN FRANCISCO
The National Archives
1000 Commodore Drive
San Bruno, CA 94066-2350
415/876-9009

The Americans United Research Foundation, the National Council on Religion and Public Education, and the National Archives welcome teachers' requests for information about educational opportunities and for assistance in preparing teaching materials and pursuing research.

1

Beyond Toleration to Freedom

An address to President George Washington from the Hebrew congregation in Newport, Rhode Island, and his reply, 1790

ocument 1

tter from Moses Seixas, Warden of Congregation Jeshuat Israel, Newport, Rhode Island, to President
rge Washington, August 17, 1790

rce: Papers of George Washington, Library of Congress, Washington, D.C.

To the President of the United States of America.

Sir

Permit the children of the Stock of Abraham to approach you with the most cordial affection and esteem for your person & merits — and to join with our fellow Citizens in welcoming you to NewPort.

With pleasure we reflect on those days — those days of difficulty, & danger when the God of Israel, who delivered David from the peril of the Sword, — Shielded Your head in the day of battle: — And we rejoice to think, that the Same Spirit, who rested in the Bosom of the greatly beloved Daniel enabling him to preside over the Provinces of the Babylonish Empire, rests and ever will rest upon you, enabling you to discharge the arduous duties of Chief Magistrate. in these States.

Deprived as we heretofore have been of the invaluable rights of free Citizens, we now (with a deep sense of gratitude to the Almighty disposer of all events) behold a Government, erected by the Majesty of the People — a Government, which to bigotry gives no Sanction, to persecution no assistance — but generously affording to All liberty of conscience, and immunities of Citizenship: — deeming every one, of whatever Nation, tongue, or Language equal parts of the great governmental Machine: — This so ample and extensive Federal Union whose basis is Philanthropy, mutual confidence and Publick Virtue, we cannot but acknowledge to be the work of the Great God, who ruleth in the Armies of Heaven and among the Inhabitants of the Earth, doing whatsoever seemeth him good.

Document 1 (continued)

For all the Blessings of civil and religious liberty which we enjoy under an equal and benign administration, we desire to send up our thanks to the Antient of Days, the great preserver of Men—beseeching him, that the Angel who conducted our forefathers through the wilderness into the promised land, may graciously conduct you through all the difficulties and dangers of this mortal life:—And, when like Joshua full of days and full of honour, you are gathered to your Fathers, may you be admitted into the Heavenly Paradise to partake of the water of life, and the tree of immortality.

Done and Signed by Order of the Hebrew Congregation in New Port Rhode Island August 17th 1790:

Moses Seixas, Warden

anscription of Document 1

tter from Moses Seixas, Warden of Congregation Jeshuat Israel, Newport, Rhode Island, to President
rge Washington, August 17, 1790

TO THE PRESIDENT OF THE UNITED STATES OF AMERICA.

Sir.

Permit the children of the stock of Abraham to approach you with the most cordial affection and esteem for your person and merits, and to join with our fellow citizens in welcoming you to Newport.

With pleasure we reflect on those days, of difficulty and danger, when the God of Israel, who delivered David from the peril of the sword,—shielded your head in the day of battle:—and we rejoice to think that the same Spirit who rested in the bosom of the greatly beloved Daniel, enabling him to preside over the Provinces of the Babylonish Empire, rests and ever will rest upon you, enabling you to discharge the arduous duties of Chief Magistrate in these States.

Deprived as we heretofore have been of the invaluable rights of free citizens, we now (with a deep sense of gratitude to the Almighty dispenser of all events) behold a Government, erected by the Majesty of the People.—a Government, which to bigotry gives no sanction, to persecution no assistance—but generously affording to All liberty of conscience, and immunities of Citizenship:—deeming every one, of whatever Nation, tongue, or language equal parts of the great governmental machine:—This so ample and extensive Federal Union whose basis is Philanthropy, mutual confidence and Publick Virtue, we cannot but acknowledge to be the work of the Great God, who ruleth in the Armies of Heaven and among the Inhabitants of the Earth, doing whatsoever seemeth him good.

For all the Blessings of civil and religious liberty which we enjoy under an equal and benign administration, we desire to send up our thanks to the ancient of days, the great preserver of men—beseeching him, that the Angel who conducted our forefathers through the wilderness into the promised land, may graciously conduct you through all the difficulties and dangers of this mortal life:—And, when like Joshua full of days and full of honour, you are gathered to your Fathers, may you be admitted into the Heavenly Paradise to partake of the water of life, and the tree of immortality.

Done and signed by order of the Hebrew Congregation in NewPort Rhode Island, August 17th, 1790.

Moses Seixas. Warden.

Document 2

A letter from President George Washington to the Hebrew Congregation in Newport, Rhode Island, August 21, 1790

Source: This document is on long-term loan to the B'nai B'rith Klutznick Museum, Washington, D.C. Used b permission of the Morganstern Foundation.

To the Hebrew Congregation in Newport
Rhode Island.

Gentlemen.

While I receive, with much satisfaction, your Address replete with expressions of affection and esteem; I rejoice in the opportunity of assuring you, that I shall always retain a grateful remembrance of the cordial welcome I experienced in my visit to Newport, from all classes of citizens.

The reflection on the days of difficulty and danger which are past is rendered the more sweet, from a consciousness that they are succeeded by days of uncommon prosperity and security. If we have wisdom to make the best use of the advantages with which we are now favored, we cannot fail, under the just administration of a good Government, to become a great and a happy people.

The Citizens of the United States of America have a right to applaud themselves for having given to mankind examples of an enlarged and liberal

cument 2 (continued)

policy: a policy worthy of imitation. All profess
alike liberty of conscience and immunities of
citizenship. It is now no more that toleration is
spoken of, as if it was by the indulgence of one
class of people, that another enjoyed the exercise
of their inherent natural rights. For happily
the

the Government of the United States, which gives to
bigotry no sanction, to persecution no assistance,
requires only that they who live under its protection,
should demean themselves as good citizens, in giving
it on all occasions their effectual support.

It would be inconsistent with the frankness
of my character not to avow that I am pleased with
your favorable opinion of my administration, and
fervent wishes for my felicity. May the children of
the Stock of Abraham, who dwell in this land, continue
to merit and enjoy the good will of the other Inhabitants;
while every one shall sit in safety under his own
vine and figtree, and there shall be none to make
him afraid. May the father of all mercies scatter
light and not darkness in our paths, and make
us all in our several vocations here, and in his
own due time and way everlastingly happy.

G. Washington

Transcription of Document 2

A letter from President George Washington to the Hebrew Congregation in Newport, Rhode Island, August 21, 1790

Gentlemen.

While I receive, with much satisfaction, your address replete with expressions of affection and esteem, I rejoice in the opportunity of assuring you, that I shall always retain a grateful remembrance of the cordial welcome I experienced in my visit to Newport, from all classes of Citizens.

The reflection on the days of difficulty and danger which are past is rendered the more sweet, from a consciousness that they are succeeded by days of uncommon prosperity and security. If we have wisdom to make the best use of the advantages with which we are now favored, we cannot fail, under the just administration of a good government, to become a great and a happy people.

The Citizens of the United States of America have a right to applaud themselves for having given to mankind examples of an enlarged and liberal policy: a policy worthy of imitation. All possess alike liberty of conscience and immunities of citizenship. It is now no more that toleration is spoken of, as if it was by the indulgence of one class of people, that another enjoyed the exercise of their inherent natural rights. For happily the Government of the United States, which gives to bigotry no sanction, to persecution no assistance, requires only that they who live under its protection should demean themselves as good citizens, in giving it on all occasions their effectual support.

It would be inconsistent with the frankness of my character not to avow that I am pleased with your favorable opinion of my administration, and fervent wishes for my felicity. May the Children of the Stock of Abraham, who dwell in this land, continue to merit and enjoy the good will of the other Inhabitants; while every one shall sit in safety under his own vine and figtree, and there shall be none to make him afraid. May the father of all mercies scatter light and not darkness in our paths, and make us all in our several vocations useful here, and in his own due time and way everlastingly happy.

G. Washington

Historical Background

During a visit to Rhode Island in 1790, President George Washington was presented with an address from the Hebrew Congregation of Newport giving thanks to God for the freedom of conscience they enjoyed in the new nation (document 1). The president replied immediately with one of the most beautiful affirmations of religious liberty in American history (document 2).

Washington's letter proclaims religious liberty for *all*, heralding a truly revolutionary experiment in freedom. "It is now no more that toleration is spoken of," he wrote, "as if it was by the indulgence of one class of people that another enjoyed the exercise of their inherent natural rights." With these words, Washington offered a vision of a nation that would for the first time in history protect liberty of conscience for people of all faiths or none. A year later, this vision of liberty shared by so many of the founding fathers would be added to the Constitution with the adoption of the Bill of Rights.

The First American Jews

The Newport Jewish community that greeted President Washington in 1790 had been in Rhode Island since 1658. In that year 15 Spanish and Portuguese Jewish families arrived in Newport, most probably from Curacao in the West Indies. These early Jewish settlers found something most rare in the history of the Jews—a place where liberty of conscience in matters of faith was guaranteed for all citizens.

The significance of the Rhode Island haven cannot be exaggerated. The Jews of Europe had suffered centuries of persecution. Periods of toleration were frequently broken by waves of tyranny. Confined to ghettos, excluded from many professions, subject to periodic massacres and expulsions, Jews had long experienced degradation and destruction throughout Europe.

The first American Jews were descendants of Spanish Jews who were expelled from Spain by royal decree in 1492. During that period, many Jews were killed and others were forced to convert to Christianity. Many "new Christians," called Marranos (swine) or *conversos* by Christians, continued to practice Judaism in private.

A number of Jews made their way to the Spanish and Portuguese colonies in the New World. There, too, they were harassed and often killed. A period of relief came in the early 17th century when the Dutch captured Portuguese Brazil. For a time, the more liberal policies of the Dutch tolerated the practice of Judaism. Many conversos returned to Judaism and hundreds of other Jews migrated to Brazil to establish the first Jewish community in the New World.

When the Portuguese recaptured Brazil in 1654, the Jews were once again forced to flee. Twenty-three Jews made their way to New Amsterdam, where they formed the first Jewish community on North American soil.

Sadly, the Jews encountered hostility even in the Dutch colony of New Amsterdam. The colony's governor, Peter Stuyvesant, supported by some of the Dutch Reformed clergy, tried to expel the new arrivals, fearing among other things that their presence would lead to toleration of "Baptists and Lutherans" as well. Overruled by the directors of the Dutch West India Company (a few of whom were Jews), Stuyvesant was forced to allow the Jews to remain. The governor did succeed, however, in denying the Jews basic rights, including the right to build a synagogue.

The "Soul Liberty" of Roger Williams

The intolerant and bigoted reception of the Jews in New Amsterdam stands in sharp contrast to the reception a second group of Jews received in Rhode Island just a few years later. These Jews, some of whom were also conversos, longed to find a land where they could practice their faith freely and openly. In Rhode Island they had finally found such a place.

The liberty of conscience that the Jews found in Rhode Island was rooted in the Puritan religious convictions of Roger Williams, the founder and first governor of the colony. Williams was a Separatist whose abiding interest was to protect the "Garden of the Church" from the "Wilderness of the World." He went further than most Puritans, insisting that the true church be free of all corruptions (including those of the Church of England). Only the "regenerate," those elected by God for salvation, were to be considered legitimate members of Christ's church.

Williams' insistence on the purity of the church led him to advocate separation of the church from all worldly contamination, including state involvement in matters of faith. This view of the church was a direct challenge to the Puritan leaders of Massachusetts Bay, who were attempting to establish a Holy Commonwealth where both church and state were subject to divine law as given in Scripture. For the Massachusetts Puritans, such a society required that the civil magistrates have responsibility for enforcing obedience to God's ordinances.

The Puritan authorities realized that the religious views of Roger Williams attacked the very foundation of their "covenant with God" to found a "New Israel." Williams preached that with the coming of Christ, God had dissolved the connection between church and state represented in the Israel of the Hebrew scriptures. In his view, God had not chosen the Puritans or anyone else to establish the divine kingdom on earth.

Williams was convinced that state involvement in the worship of God is contrary to the divine will and inevitably leads to defilement of the church. Only a church free from state interference can be a voluntary association of God's people. Every individual, he insisted, must remain free to follow the dictates of conscience in matters of faith.

Citing Europe's long history of religious persecutions, Williams pointed out that coercion in matters of faith inevitably leads to bloodshed, and forced conversion ends in hypocrisy. All people must be allowed what he called "soul liberty," even if they err, because only a free conscience has even the possibility of knowing the truth. In his famous *Bloody Tenet of Persecution* (1644), Williams made the point this way:

> [I]t is the will and command of God that (since the coming of his son the Lord Jesus) a permission of the most paganish, Jewish, Turkish, or antichristian consciences and worships, be granted to all men in all nations and countries; and they are only to be fought against with that sword which is only (in soul matters) able to conquer, to wit, the sword of God's spirit, the Word of God.

Williams' arguments in favor of soul liberty challenged the authority of Puritan magistrates to enforce biblical law in religious matters. For this and other "heretical" views, Williams was banished from Massachusetts Bay in 1635. A year later he founded the colony of Rhode Island and began his "lively experiment" in soul liberty.

Rhode Island broke dramatically with the past to become the first colony with no established church and the first society in America to grant liberty of conscience to people of all faiths. Jews, Quakers, and others not welcome elsewhere made their home there.

Few people in the 17th century imagined that Williams' radical experiment could succeed. A society without divine sanction, especially one that allowed religious dissent, appeared to most observers to have no chance for survival. After refusing entry to a shipload of Quakers in 1657, a group of Dutch Reformed ministers in New Amsterdam offered this assessment of Rhode Island:

> We suppose they [the Quakers] went to Rhode Island, for that is the receptacle of all sorts of riff-raff people and is nothing less that the sewer . . . of New England. All of the cranks of New England retire thither . . . They are not tolerated . . . in any other place (Rhode Island Committee for the Humanities 1986).

Actually, the Quakers were not exactly "tolerated" in Rhode Island. They were given something greater: full freedom to follow the dictates of their consciences in worship and belief. Roger Williams was committed to soul liberty, not toleration. Convinced of the truth of his own views of scripture, Williams scorned the Quakers and their conviction about the guidance they claimed to receive from an "inner light." What is important, however, is that Williams' opposition to other faiths did not affect his deep commitment to liberty of conscience for people of all faiths or none. All were welcome in Rhode Island because Williams believed that God wished all to be granted freedom of conscience, no matter how heretical he took their religious views to be.

The Jews of Newport

The Jews who found safe harbor in Rhode Island were soon joined by others to form the second largest Jewish community after New Amsterdam. For the first hundred years, the Newport Congregation worshipped in private homes. In 1759 the Congregation decided to build a synagogue, and in 1763 America's oldest surviving Jewish house of worship, the Touro Synagogue, was dedicated.

When Washington visited Newport in 1790, the Jewish community there had dwindled to a small number. Many of Newport's citizens had been forced to leave due to economic decline in the city during the years following the Revolution. Touro Synagogue closed a few years after Washington's visit and was not reopened for worship on a permanent basis until 1883. By the end of the 19th century, waves of immigration from Europe had once again brought Jews to Newport.

President Washington's Response

George Washington was a lifelong advocate of liberty of conscience. The affirmation of full religious liberty given in his response to the address of the Newport Congregation was echoed in letters he wrote through the years to many religious groups. In all of these letters, he is careful to show equal appreciation and respect toward all faiths. Nowhere does he discuss his own religious views or affiliation.

Washington made clear to the Jews of Newport his view that religious liberty is a "natural right." In another letter, this one to the much-persecuted Quakers, Washington amplified his view that religious liberty is a basic right of every individual:

> The liberty enjoyed by the people of these States, of worshipping Almighty God agreeably to their consciences, is not only among the choicest of their *blessings*, but also of their *rights*. While men perform their social duties faithfully, they do all that society or the state can with propriety demand or expect; and remain responsible only to their Maker for the religion, or modes of faith, which they may prefer or profess.

The state, in short, may not grant or remove our inalienable right to freedom of conscience.

President Washington also gave assurances of freedom to Roman Catholics, members of a church viewed with great antagonism by many Protestants in the United States of 1790:

> As mankind become more liberal, they will be more apt to allow, that all those who conduct themselves as worthy members of the community are equally entitled to the protection of civil government. I hope ever to see America among the foremost nations in examples of justice and liberality. And I presume, that your fellow-citizens will not forget the patriotic part which you took in the accomplishment of their revolution, and the establishment of their government; or the important assistance, which they received, from a Nation in which the Roman Catholic religion is professed. . . .

Significantly, all of these letters were written before the adoption of the Bill of Rights in 1791. President Washington clearly believed that the Constitution already protected liberty of conscience. To the Baptists of Virginia he wrote in 1789:

> If I could have entertained the slightest apprehension, that the constitution framed in the convention, where I had the honor to preside, might possibly endanger the religious rights of any ecclesiastical society, certainly I would never have placed my signature to it; and if I could now conceive that the general government might ever be so administered as to render the liberty of conscience insecure, I beg you will be persuaded, that no one would be more zealous than myself to establish effectual barriers against the horrors of spiritual tyranny, and every species of religious persecution. For you doubtless remember, that I have often expressed my sentiments that every man, conducting himself as a good citizen, and being accountable to God alone for his religious opinions, ought to be protected in worshipping the Deity according to the dictates of his own conscience.

Baptists, Quakers, Catholics, and Jews must have received the words of President Washington with great joy and a sense of relief. All had experienced persecution in the New World and all, including the Puritans and Anglicans, had experienced persecution in Europe. For the Jews, however, victims of oppression and tyranny for so many centuries, Washington's words must have been especially sweet. As they put it their address:

> Deprived as we heretofore have been of the invaluable rights of free citizens, we now (with a deep sense of gratitude to the Almighty Dispenser of all Events) behold a Government erected by the majesty of the people, a Government which gives to bigotry no sanction to persecution no assistance; but generously affording to all liberty of conscience and immunities of citizenship, deeming everyone, of whatever nation, tongue, or language, equal parts of the great Government machine.

In his reply, Washington endorsed the Congregation's definition of a government that "gives to bigotry no sanction, to persecution no assistance." But he went much further, telling the Jews that liberty of conscience is not a gift of the government, but their "inherent natural right."

This full liberty of conscience, so movingly espoused by the "Father of our country," remains the first principle of the American way of life. For the first time in history, a nation committed itself to move beyond persecution, and even beyond toleration, to "free exercise" of religion. Though America's history has been marred by outbreaks of persecution and religious bigotry, the United States has achieved a degree of religious liberty unprecedented in the world's history. Religious liberty, freedom of conscience, remains America's greatest gift to world civilization.

References

Rhode Island Committee for the Humanities. (1986). *The Legacy of Roger Williams*.

Suggestions for Using the Documents

Discussion Questions

1. What is the difference between "toleration" and "free exercise of religion?" Why was this distinction particularly significant for the first American Jews?
2. How does Roger Williams' conception of "soul liberty" differ from other ideas of liberty?
3. What is the meaning of the phrase "inherent natural rights"? What are our natural rights?
4. Why did most societies of the 17th century view freedom of conscience for people of all faiths or none as a dangerous idea?
5. Religious liberty or freedom of conscience has been called America's "first liberty." Why?
6. Although religious liberty is guaranteed by the First Amendment, has America always lived up to this ideal? Discuss positive and negative chapters in America's experiment with religious liberty.

Extension Activities

1. Assign four students to prepare brief oral reports about the biblical characters mentioned in the Hebrew Congregation's letter (Abraham, David, Daniel, and Joshua). After the reports are given, have the class discuss how each of these characters is used in the letter. What is the point being made in each case?
2. President Washington ends his letter with a quote from the Hebrew scriptures (Micah 4:4). Ask the class if anyone recognizes the reference. If not, send the class on a detective hunt to find the source and identify the exact text.
3. Ask students to discuss with their parents the Hebrew Congregation's letter and Washington's reply. How has religious liberty, or freedom of conscience, been important in their lives or the lives of their ancestors?

Research Topics

1. What were the religious convictions of George Washington?
2. Why were the Jews persecuted in Europe for centuries?
3. Baptists consider Roger Williams one of their founding fathers. How did Williams shape the Baptist view of religious liberty?
4. Investigate the history of the Jewish community in Newport, Rhode Island. What is the status of the congregation there today?
5. When and how did the Jews of New Amsterdam finally enjoy full religious liberty?

Additional Resources

Cousins, Norman, ed. (1958). *In God We Trust: The Religious Beliefs and Ideas of the American Founding Fathers.* New York: Harper and Brothers. A useful collection of writings concerning religion by Washington and other Founding Fathers.

In Search of Tolerance. (1978). Del Mar, Calif.: McGraw-Hill. A film that discusses the European background of religious groups whose search for freedom brought them to America. Includes Anabaptists, Huguenots, Puritans, and Quakers.

Jews in America. (1973). New York: Anti-Defamation League. A two-part filmstrip and discussion guide covering 300 years of Jewish life in the U.S.

Morgan, Edmund. (1987). *Roger Williams: The Church and State.* New York: W. W. Norton. The best discussion of Roger Williams' views on religious liberty.

Religious Freedom in America's Beginnings. (1971). Dearfield, Ill.: Coronet Films. This 14-minute film gives a concise overview of the origins of religious liberty in colonial America.

Ruderman, Jerome. (1974). *Jews in American History: A Teacher's Guide.* New York: Anti-Defamation League. An excellent resource for teaching about the role of Jews in the development of the United States. Each chapter includes discussion questions, student activities, and a bibliography of books and audiovisual materials.

Touro Synagogue, the place of worship for the Jews of Newport, Rhode Island since 1763, is also a National Historic Site that may be visited throughout the year. For more information write to Touro Synagogue, 85 Touro St., Newport, R.I. 02840.

2

How High a Wall?

A letter from the Danbury Baptist
Association to President Thomas Jefferson,
1801, and his reply, 1802

ocument 3

tter from the Danbury Baptist Association to President Thomas Jefferson, October 7, 1801

rce: Papers of Thomas Jefferson, Library of Congress, Washington, D.C.

Document 3 (continued)

laws & usages, & such still are; that Religion is considered as the first object of Legislation; & therefore what religious privileges we enjoy (as a minor part of the State) we enjoy as favors granted, and not as inalienable rights: and these favors we receive at the expense of such degrading acknowledgements, as inconsistent with the rights of freemen. It is not to be wondered at therefore; if those who seek after power & gain under the pretence of government & Religion should reproach their fellow men — should reproach their chief Magistrate, as an enemy of religion law & good order because he will not, dares not assume the prerogative of Jehovah and make Laws to govern the Kingdom of Christ.

Sir, we are sensible that the President of the united States, is not the national Legislator, & also sensible that the national government cannot destroy the Laws of each State; but our hopes are strong that the sentiments of our beloved President, which have had such genial Effect already, like the radiant beams of the Sun, will shine & prevail through all these States and all the world till Hierarchy and Tyranny be destroyed from the Earth. Sir, when we reflect on your past services, and see a glow of philanthic joy and good will shining forth in a course of more than thirty years we have reason to believe that Americas God has raised you up to fill the chair

ocument 3 (continued)

of State out of that good will which he bears to
the Millions which you preside over. May God
strengthen you for the arduous task which providence
& the voice of the people have call you to sustain
and support you in your Administration against
all the predetermind opposition of those who wish
to rise to wealth & importance on the poverty and
subjection of the people ————

And may the Lord preserve you safe from every
evil and bring you at last to his Heavenly Kingdom
through Jesus Christ our Glorious Mediator.

Signed in behalf of the Association.
                                    Neh.h Dodge   } The Committee
                                    Ephm Robbins
                                    Stephen S. Nelson

Transcription of Document 3

A letter from the Danbury Baptist Association to President Thomas Jefferson, October 7, 1801

The address of the Danbury Baptist Association in the State of Connecticut, assembled October 7, 180
To Thomas Jefferson the President of the United States of America

Sir,

Among the many millions in America and Europe who rejoice in your Election to office, we embrace the first opportunity which we have enjoyed in our collective capacity, since your Inauguration, to express our great satisfaction, in your appointment to the chief Magistracy in the United States: And though our mode of expression may be less courtly and pompous than what many others clothe their addresses with, we beg you, sir to Believe, that none are more sincere.

Our Sentiments are uniformly on the side of Religious Liberty—That Religion is at all times and places a Matter between God and Individuals—That no man ought to suffer in Name, person or effects on account of his religious Opinions—That the legitimate Power of civil Government extends no further than to punish the man who works ill to his neighbors: But Sir our constitution of government is not specific. Our national charter, together with the Laws made coincident therewith, were adopted as the Basis of our government at the time of our revolution; and such had been our laws & usages, & such still are; that Religion is considered as the first object of Legislation; & therefore what religious privileges we enjoy (as a minor part of the State) we enjoy as favors granted, and not as inalienable rights: and these favors we receive at the expense of such degrading acknowledgements, as are inconsistent with the rights of freemen. It is not to be wondered at therefore; if those who seek power & gain under the pretence of government & Religion should reproach their fellowmen— should reproach their chief Magistrate, as an enemy of religion Law & good order because he will not, dares not assume the prerogative of Jehovah and make Laws to govern the Kingdom of Christ.

Sir, we are sensible that the President of the united States is not the national Legislator, & also sensible that the national government cannot destroy the Laws of each State; but our hopes are strong that the sentiments of our beloved President, which have had such genial affect already, like the radiant beams of the Sun, will shine and prevail through all these States and all the world till Hierarchy and Tyranny be destroyed from the Earth. Sir, when we reflect on your past services and see a glow of philanthropy and good will shining forth in a course of more than thirty years we have reason to believe that America's God has raised you up to fill the chair of State out of the good will which he bears to the Millions which you preside over. May God strengthen you for the arduous task which providence & the voice of the people have called you to sustain and support you in your Administration against all the predetermined opposition of those who wish to rise to wealth & importance on the poverty and subjection of the people.

And may the Lord preserve you safe from every evil and bring you at last to his Heavenly Kingdom through Jesus Christ our Glorious Mediator.

Signed on behalf of the Association . . . The Committee

Nehr Dodge
Ephraim Robbins
Stephen S. Nelson

Document 4

A letter from Thomas Jefferson to the Danbury Baptist Association, January 1, 1802
Source: Papers of Thomas Jefferson, Library of Congress, Washington, D.C.

cument 4 (continued)

science, I shall see with sincere satisfaction the progress of those sentiments which tend to restore to man all his natural rights, convinced he has no natural right in opposition to his social duties.

I reciprocate your kind prayers for the protection & blessing of the common father and creator of man, and tender you for yourselves & your religious association, assurances of my high respect & esteem.

Th. Jefferson

Jan. 1. 1802.

Transcription of Document 4

A letter from Thomas Jefferson to the Danbury Baptist Association, January 1, 1802

To mess. Nehemiah Dodge, Ephraim Robbins, & Stephen S. Nelson, a committee of the Danbury Bapt association in the state of Connecticut.

Gentlemen

The affectionate sentiments of esteem and approbation which you are so good as to express towards me, on behalf of the Danbury Baptist association, give me the highest satisfaction, my duties dictate a faithful & zealous pursuit of the interests of my constituents, & in recognition as they are persuaded of my fidelity to these duties, the discharge of them becomes more and more pleasing.

Believing with you that religion is a matter which lies solely between Man & his God, that he owes account to none other for his faith or his worship, that the legitimate powers of government reach actions only, & not opinions. I contemplate with sovereign reverence that act of the whole American people which declared that *their* legislature should "make no law regarding an establishment of religion, or prohibiting the free exercise thereof," thus building a wall of separation between Church & State. Adhering to this expression of the supreme will of the nation in behalf of the rights of conscience, I shall see with sincere satisfaction the progress of those sentiments which tend to restore to men all his natural rights, convinced he has no natural right in opposition to his social duties.

I reciprocate your kind prayers for the protection & blessing of the common father and creator of man, and tender you for yourselves & your religious association, assurances of my high respect & esteem.

T. W. Jefferson
Jan. 1. 1802.

Historical Background

The famous "wall of separation" metaphor used by Thomas Jefferson to describe the First Amendment is contained in an 1802 letter he wrote as president to the Baptists of Danbury, Connecticut (document 4). Though the metaphor is widely quoted and debated, most notably in key Supreme Court opinions, the context for Jefferson's original letter is rarely discussed or understood. A closer look at both Jefferson's letter and the address from the Baptists that precipitated it (document 3), reveals much about Jefferson's views concerning the First Amendment as well as the early development of religious liberty in the United States.

The Baptist "Wall of Separation"

When the Danbury Baptists wrote to President Jefferson in 1801, the Religious Liberty clauses of the First Amendment had been part of the Constitution for nearly a decade. The No Establishment Clause, however, applied only to the federal government, leaving the states free to establish religion. In 1801, a few states, including Connecticut, still maintained church establishments. Not until disestablishment in Massachusetts in 1833 was the United States free from state-supported churches.

Connecticut was founded by Puritans who sought to create a society ruled by divine law as given in the Bible. The religious freedom they desired was freedom for themselves to live and worship as God commanded. They were convinced that such a "holy commonwealth" required that their faith, represented in the Congregational churches, be supported and protected by the state.

As preservers of the true faith and builders of a "new Israel," the Puritans of Connecticut enacted laws against heresy and moved to banish dissenters. In the early 18th century, fears that the king of England might attempt to exercise more power over their colony pushed Connecticut to grant a measure of toleration to some dissenting groups. By the time of the Revolution, the Congregational establishment had given way to a multiple establishment that allowed for tax money to be used in support of those denominations that gained the support of the majority of voters in each town. Members of dissenting groups, such as the Baptists, could be exempt from payment of these taxes by certifying membership in a dissenting church.

Baptists, however, were not content with this form of establishment. Local communities often made it difficult for Baptists to certify their membership in a Baptist church, and the established churches enjoyed privileges not granted to the minority faiths.

As spiritual descendants of Roger Williams, the Baptists believed that religion must be entirely voluntary and that the state had no right to interfere in matters of faith. In their letter to Jefferson, the Danbury Baptists defined religious liberty in theological terms that separate the free exercise of religion from the power of the state:

> Our Sentiments are uniformly on the side of Religious Liberty—That Religion is at all times and places a Matter between God and Individuals—That no man ought to suffer in Name, person or effects on account of his religious Opinions—That the legitimate Power of civil Government extends no further than to punish the man who *works ill to his neighbors.* . . .

The basis for the Baptists' argument was their belief that religion cannot be mandated or controlled by the state because God has created the conscience free to choose for or against God. Thus, religious liberty is not a favor that can be granted by legislation, as in Connecticut, because it is "an inalienable right," a right given by the Creator.

The Baptists of Connecticut deeply resented a legislature that presumed to pass laws regulating churches and taxing citizens for the support of religion. They bitterly complained to Jefferson that "what religious privileges we enjoy" as a minority faith are "as favors granted." Such interference with faith and worship was a "degrading" attempt by the state to come between Christ and his people.

The Danbury Baptists sought the same liberty of conscience and church-state separation that Roger Williams demanded of his fellow Puritans in 1631. Like Williams, who himself was a Baptist for a short time, the Danbury Association protested the tyranny of a state that "assumes the prerogative of Jehovah" to "make Laws to govern the Kingdom of Christ." Long before Jefferson, Williams had used the "wall of separation" metaphor to express the view, later adopted by other dissenters, that state interference in matters of faith led only to the corruption of Christ's church:

> When they have opened a gap in the hedge or wall of separation between the garden of the church and the wilderness of the world, God hath ever broke down the wall itself, removed the candlestick, and made His garden a wilderness, as at this day (Howe 1965).

Jefferson and the Baptists

The Baptists of Connecticut had good reason to hope that the election of Thomas Jefferson to the presidency would further the cause of disestablishment and religious liberty. He was, after all, the author of the Virginia Statute for Religious Freedom, the bill that disestablished religion in Virginia and greatly influenced the shaping of the Religious Liberty clauses of the First Amendment.

In the battle for disestablishment in Virginia, the Baptists had allied themselves with the rationalists Thomas Jefferson and James Madison. Baptist preachers in Virginia were well aware of persecution by established churches, some of their number having served time in prison for spreading the gospel in ways not approved by the state. Their strong opposition in 1785 to the General Assessment (using tax money to support the salary of clergy) helped to defeat that bill and pave the way for passage of Jefferson's statute.

The alliance of Jefferson and the Baptists did not signal agreement about matters of faith. Jefferson, a son of the Enlightenment, put his faith in human reason to understand and accept the truth. The revivals and conversions of the Baptists, not to mention the content of their convictions, were elements of religion far removed from the rationalistic Deism of Jefferson.

Jefferson and the Baptists did agree, however, that freedom of conscience is an inalienable right not subject to the power of any state to grant or deny. Faith must be chosen, not coerced. Thus the state must be separated from the church and the voluntary way in religion encouraged.

President Jefferson's Famous Reply

The significance of Thomas Jefferson's response to the Danbury Baptists is a much-debated issue. Does it represent the considered views of one of our Founding Fathers on the meaning of the Religious Liberty clauses of the First Amendment? Or is it simply the conventional response of a busy president to one of the many congratulatory addresses he received?

Jefferson turned his attention to the Baptist letter on January 1, 1802. As the following note to Attorney General Levi Lincoln makes clear, he decided to use his answer as an opportunity to express his views on church-state questions:

> Adverse to receive addresses, yet unable to prevent them, I have generally endeavored to turn them to some account, by making them the occasion, by way of answer, of sowing useful truths and principles among the people, which might germinate and become rooted among their political tenets. The Baptist address, now enclosed, admits of a condemnation of the alliance between Church and State, under the authority of the Constitution. It furnishes an occasion, too, which I have long wished to find, of saying why I do not proclaim fastings and thanksgivings, as my predecessors did. The address, to be sure, does not point at this, and its introduction is awkward. But I foresee no opportunity of doing it more pertinently. I know it will give great offence to the New England clergy; but the

advocate of religious freedom is to expect neither peace nor forgiveness from them. Will you be so good as to examine the answer, and suggest any alterations which might prevent an ill effect, or promote a good one, among the people? You understand the temper of those in the North, and can weaken it, therefore, to their stomachs: it is at present seasoned to the Southern taste only. I would ask the favor of you to return it, with the address, in the course of the day or evening. Health and affection (Papers of Thomas Jefferson).

The draft reviewed by the attorney general did in fact contain language explaining why Jefferson did not proclaim days of fasting and thanksgiving. After the well-known line about the "wall of separation," Jefferson originally wrote:

> Congress thus inhibited from acts respecting religion, and the Executive authorized only to execute their acts, I have refrained from prescribing even occasional performances of devotion. . . .

He also added language, later removed, stating that religious exercises should be subject only to "the voluntary regulations and discipline of each respective sect."

After receiving Levi Lincoln's advice that such statements might prove politically damaging in New England, Jefferson eliminated that section. In the draft letter, Jefferson notes in the margin that

> this paragraph was omitted on the suggestion that it might give uneasiness to some of our republican friends in the eastern states where the proclamation of thanksgivings etc. by their Executive is an [word obscured] and habit and is respected.

It might be concluded from this evidence that President Jefferson's letter was not a conventional response. He took the occasion of answering the Danbury Baptists as an opportunity to air his views on the separation of church and state, though he drew back for political reasons from an even more forceful statement. In a line he did not cut, he made very clear that he wished to encourage disestablishment in Connecticut, viewing state establishment of religion as a violation of basic human rights:

> Adhering to this expression of the supreme will of the nation in behalf of the rights of conscience, I shall see with sincere satisfaction the progress of those sentiments which tend to restore to man all his natural rights, convinced he has no natural right in opposition to his social duties.

The Supreme Court and the "Wall of Separation"

The first use by the Supreme Court of Jefferson's letter to the Baptists came in the landmark "free exercise" case, *Reynolds v. United States* in 1878. In that case, the Court upheld the conviction of George Reynolds, secretary to Brigham Young, for polygamy, thus setting a limit on the free exercise of the Mormon faith. Chief Justice Waite, writing for the Court, quoted Jefferson's letter in support of the Court's interpretation of the First Amendment. He then added:

> Coming as this does from an acknowledged leader of the advocates of the measure [the First Amendment], it may be accepted almost as an authoritative declaration of the scope and effect of the amendment thus secured. Congress was deprived of all legislative power over mere opinion, but was left free to reach actions which were in violation of social duties or subversive of good order.

Note that the first use of Jefferson's letter by the Court had less to do with the "wall of separation" and more to do with the distinction Jefferson makes between actions and opinions in matters of religion. The Court used Jefferson's words, "the legislative powers of the Government reach actions only, and not opinions," to support its view that the government may set limits on actions, even those motivated by religious belief. Later Supreme Court decisions refined the distinction, requiring, among other things, that the state show "compelling interest" before interfering with religious practice. Nevertheless, following *Reynolds*, the "wall" would never be high enough to prohibit governmental limitation on the "exercise" in the free exercise clause.

The best-known use of Jefferson's letter was in the majority opinion written by Hugo Black in *Everson v. Board of Education* in 1947. In a 5–4 decision, the Court upheld the practice of reimbursing parents of parochial school children for money spent to reach school on public buses. The Court denied that such reimbursements constituted state aid to religion, arguing that public transportation of school children was a public benefit that the state had extended to all students without regard to their religious belief.

In deciding the *Everson* case, the majority of the Court took the opportunity to interpret in the strongest terms the meaning of the No Establishment Clause of the First Amendment. Noting that the First Amendment was applicable to the states by the Fourteenth Amendment, the Court employed Jefferson's metaphor to build a high wall of separation:

> The "establishment of religion" clause of the First Amendment means at least this: Neither a state nor the Federal Government can set up a church. Neither can pass laws which aid one religion, aid all religions, or prefer one religion over another. Neither can force nor influence a person to go or to remain away from church against his

will or force him to profess a belief or disbelief in any religion. No person can be punished for entertaining or professing religious beliefs or disbeliefs, for church attendance or non-attendance. No tax in any amount, large or small, can be levied to support any religious activities or institutions, whatever form they may be called, or whatever form they may adopt to teach or practice religion. Neither a state nor the Federal Government can, openly or secretly, participate in the affairs of any religious organizations or groups and vice versa. In the words of Jefferson, the clause against the establishment of religion by law was intended to erect "a wall of separation between Church and State."

Subsequent Supreme Court decisions, notably *Illinois ex rel. McCollum v. Board of Education* (1948) and *Engel v. Vitale* (1962), make liberal use of Jefferson's wall. Dissenting Justices objected that the "wall of separation" was an inappropriate and misleading image for interpreting the No Establishment Clause. In the *Vitale* school prayer case, Justice Stewart dissented from the majority opinion striking down state-sponsored school prayer with a direct attack on the use of Jefferson's metaphor:

> I think that the Court's task, in this as in all areas of constitutional adjudication, is not responsibly aided by the uncritical invocation of metaphors like "the wall of separation," a phrase nowhere to be found in the Constitution. What is relevant to the issue here is . . . the history of the religious traditions of our people, reflected in countless practices of the institutions and officials of our government.

The most blistering attack on the use of Thomas Jefferson's metaphor came in the dissent of Justice William Rehnquist in *Wallace v. Jaffree* in 1985. In that case, the Court held Alabama's law authorizing a moment of silence in public schools unconstitutional. Strongly dissenting, Rehnquist argued that nothing in the No Establishment Clause, properly understood, "requires government to be strictly neutral between religion and irreligion, nor does that Clause prohibit Congress or the States from pursuing legitimate secular ends through non-discriminatory sectarian means. . . ."

Rehnquist called for a complete rethinking of the Court's approach to the No Establishment Clause, wrongly based for 40 years on "Jefferson's misleading metaphor." The letter to the Danbury Baptist Association, according to Rehnquist, "was a short note of courtesy, written 14 years after the amendments were passed by Congress." The "wall" image should be given up entirely:

> The "wall of separation between church and State" is a metaphor based on bad history, a metaphor which has proved useless as a guide to judging. It should be frankly and explicitly abandoned.

Despite repeated objections from a minority on the Court, Thomas Jefferson's views have played a central role in shaping the Court's interpretation of the No Establishment Clause. William Lee Miller, professor of religious studies at the University of Virginia, recently offered this summary of Jefferson's wall of separation:

> Did this liberty of belief for Jefferson and Madison entail separation of church and state? Yes. A ban on tax aid to religion? Yes. On state help to religion? Yes. Even religion-in-general? Yes. Even if it were extended without any favoritism among religious groups? Yes. The completely voluntary way in religion? Yes. Did all the founders agree with Jefferson and Madison? Certainly not. Otherwise there wouldn't have been a fight (Miller 1986).

A Significant Metaphor

Whatever its merits or limitations, Mr. Jefferson's (and Mr. Williams') metaphor continues to play a significant role in the debate over the meaning of the Religious Liberty clauses of the First Amendment. "Strict separationists" continue to advocate the "high and impregnable" wall between church and state envisioned by the majority in *Everson*. Many "accomodationists" work for a more porous wall, one that would allow, for example, nonpreferential government aid to religious groups.

What is most significant about these debates is that despite differing interpretations, the broad consensus in America remains: no national or state church can ever be established and no government can prefer one religious group over others. Americans ought never to forget that disestablishment in the United States separated church and state for the first time in history, making possible humanity's greatest experiment in religious liberty. Our disagreements over the size and shape of the "wall" do not obscure that remarkable achievement.

References
Howe, Mark DeWolfe. (1965). The Garden of the Wilderness: Religion and Government in American Constitutional History. Chicago: University of Chicago Press.
Papers of Thomas Jefferson. Washington, D.C.: Library of Congress. Miller, William Lee. (September 29, 1986). *Washington Post*.

Suggestions for Using the Documents

Discussion Questions

1. Why do the Baptists insist on no state interference and the "voluntary way" in matters of faith?
2. In 1801, citizens of Connecticut were debating the pros and cons of disestablishment. What do you think were the most important arguments for and against state support for religions?
3. Thomas Jefferson was in France when the First Amendment was written. Why, then, have his views been of such importance in Supreme Court interpretations of the First Amendment's religious liberty clauses? Should they be given so much weight?
4. Do you agree with Jefferson that religious liberty depends on separation of church and state? Why or why not?
5. Why was President Jefferson unable to offer more than moral support for disestablishment in Connecticut?
6. Could Connecticut or any other state establish religion today by giving state support to the clergy of selected faiths?

Extension Activities

1. Have a debate between the "separationists" and the "accomodationists." Both sides must appeal to the history of the formation of the First Amendment.
2. Have the class discuss in small groups case studies of recent church-state issues. How high a wall should be built between the church and state?

Research Topics

1. Trace the battle for disestablishment in Connecticut. Why did Congregationists eventually join with others in the support of religious liberty?
2. What role did the Baptists and other "dissenting" religious groups play in the battle for disestablishment in Virginia?
3. What can be learned about the battle for disestablishment in America from the correspondence between Thomas Jefferson and James Madison?
4. Has disestablishment aided or hurt religion in the United States? Give examples to support your answer.
5. Compare disestablishment in the United States with other nations that retain an established faith. Which approach works better? Why?

6. Who were the founders of the Baptist movement in the United States and why did they insist on separation of church and state?

Additional Resources

Commager, Henry Steele. (1975). *Jefferson, Nationalism, and the Enlightenment: Spread of Enlightenment from Old World to New.* Discusses the philosophical roots of Jefferson's thinking.

McLoughlin, William. (1971). *New England Dissent, 1630–1833: The Baptists and the Separation of Church and State.* Center for the Study of the History of Liberty in America Series. Cambridge, Mass.: Harvard University Press. A good discussion of the Baptists and religious liberty.

Miller, William L. (1986) *First Liberty: Religion and the American Public.* New York: Alfred. A. Knopf. An excellent examination of the origins of the First Amendment's religious liberty clauses.

3

The Westward Expansion of the Shakers

Excerpts from the Molly Goodrich Journal, 1805–1831

cument 5

rpts from the Molly Goodrich Journal, 1805–1831

ce: Library of Congress, Washington, D.C.

**Excerpt
A**

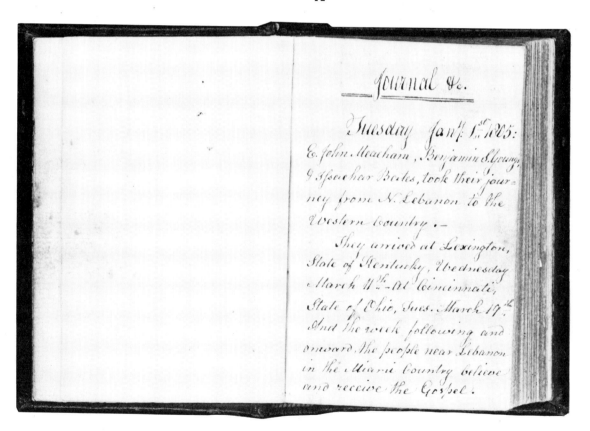

Document 5 (continued)

Excerpt B

and Kentucky. — Their horses'
ears & tails cut off near Danville, Mon. Nov. 11th at night. —
B. W. Stone the preacher at
Cane Ridge, shut his door agai[nst]
them, Mon. Nov. 25th. — Some
receive the Gospel in Mason,
the last week in November. —
They ret.d to Miami, Thu. Dec.r 5th

Mon. Dec.r 9th Daniel,
Benjamin & Malcham set
out for Beulah. Ret.d Wed.
11th & in the night Malcham's
house beset & windows broke.

'Mon. Dec.r 30th Benjamin
Issachar & Richard set out for
Eagle C.o & Kentucky. — The first
week in Feb.y 1806. the people
at Paint Lick in Garrard Co.
Ky. obey the Gospel, having be-
lieved nearly a year. The
Brethren ret.d to Turtle Creek
Wed. March 12th 1806.

Wed. March 26th 1806.
Benjamin, Issachar & Richard
set out for Beulah. — The people
there obey the Gospel having believed ab.t a year. — Breth.n ret.d
Tues. May 4th.

Excerpt C

there believe & receive the
Gospel. — Benjamin & other
Brethren ret.d to Miami.
Fri. August 2.d

Mon. June 29th E. David,
Solomon King & Daniel
Moseley, arrived at Miami
They left N.L. Mon. June 1.st

Thu. August 8th Benja—
Malcham & Richard set
out for Kentucky by Eagle C.
The 3.d week in August the
people at Shawanoe Run in

Mercer County, Ky. believe
& receive the Gospel; and the
week following, those in Shelby.
Benjamin ret.d to Miami
Thu. Sept. 19th. Rich.d & Malcham
having ret.d separately before.

Thu. Sept. 26th Issachar set
out for N.L. At night the
wicked burnt down the Believers Stand. Issachar ret.d to
Miami Tue. Dec.r 12th.

'Wed. Oct. 9th E. John and
Benjamin set out for Eagle C.
and.

ocument 5 (continued)

Excerpt D

Wed. July 18th 1810. Ishachar & John Rankin set out for Busero & Kentucky. Ishachar ret. with Joseph. March 20th 1811.

Tues. August 14th I set out for Kentucky, in company with Lucy Bacon, Maleham, Calvin, Polly Thomas & Rosanna Shields — ret. (with Constant) Tues. Sept. 3d.

Fri. August 24th Eliab & William (with Matthew H.) ret. from Kentucky.

Mon. August 27th. This day an extraordinary Mob consisting of upwards of 600 armed men, came against the Believers, in order to force them to renounce their faith or quit the country.

Thu. Sept. 13th Eliab, William & Constant start for N. Lebanon. At the same time, Archabald, Benjamin & Calvin set out for Busero, & go & return thro' y wilderness, & arrive again Tues. Dec. 4th.

Excerpt E

Tues. Sept 9. 1810. E. David, M. Ruth, & Solomon & E. Hortensia at South Union and started again for home on Thur. Sept. 17.

Mon. Jany. 4. 1819. John Meigs starts for West Union to assist for a while in the Deacons line. — and returned

Thur. Feby. 11. 1819. Joseph Allen starts for U. Village on his return to the East.

Thur. June 17 1819. The President James Monroe, and Genl. Andrew Jackson, & suits dined at South Union.

Wed. June 30. 1819. The Believers at South Union abolished slavery.

Tues. Oct. 5. 1819. I set out for Union Village in company with John McComb & Caty Rubart. Ret. Nov. 7.

Sun. Jany. 2d 1820. E. Ishachar & Wm. Davis arrived from West Union. — Ret. Jany. 13.

Document 5 (continued)

Excerpt F

Mon. Sep. 17th at U. Village, met a company of friends from South Union, Sister Mercy & Mary Naylor, Jesse McComb, & Benj. Goodhope. Stay at U. Vil. 6 days.

Monday Sep. 24th our whole South Union company, in 3 carriages, left Union Village & arrive at P. Hill, Thu. Sep. 27th. Stay at P. Hill 5 days. —

Wed. October 3d. Our whole company, 9 in number, left P. Hill & all arrived home at South Union in good health, good union, & fine spirits, on Sunday, P.M. Oct. 7th & Received a kind welcome home.

Thus ended our long journey of 1155 miles & the long anticipated visit to my native country & our gospel friends in the East. Gone 5 months 8 days.

South Union, Thu. May 22. 1828. E. Benjamin, starts for P. Hill by particular request, on account of the late law passed against the believers of this State by the Legislature last winter & to assist Eleazar in publishing a remonstrance. E. Benjamin went in a Dearborn & took Robinson Evans for company, & returned home, Sunday, June 22: & brought along the New publicatication called "Investigator".

Thur. August 21st. E. Benjamin set out with Eli McLean for Nashville, & Franklin, in Tennesse, to settle the last business of Willie W. Jones with his agent John H. Eaton — & ret. Thur. Aug. 28.

Excerpt G

Friday August 6th 1830. Eleazar arrived here from P. Hill to know how a suit brought against the believers by John Boon, would be coming on. He returned for P. Hill & U. Village in company with Francis Whyte, Wed. Aug. 25.

Note. E. Benjamin, & Eleazar, & 8 or 10 brethren more, and 8 sisters, attended court at Russellville, Tues. Aug. 10th. The Court decided that the case should be continued to the next November term, & so all the brethren & sisters returned home (in 4 carriages) on Wed. evening August 11th.

Tues. Oct. 12th. 1830, & the 3 following days, the Church Covenant at South Union signed. —

Frid. Oct. 15th. Francis and Eleazar return from Union Village & P. Hill: And, Sunday, Oct. 17. Francis spoke beautifully in public, as well as in private meetings—but behold! within 18 hours after this, he closed his eyes in peace, & departed this life into the world of Spirit, the "realms up above"—a world far better than this! — And Eleazar, after — attending the court, at

cument 5 (continued)

Excerpt
H

at Russellville in company
with E. Benjamin, & the rest,
& paying all his visits at
South Union, departed for
Union Village in the Mail
Stage, and starts from the Office
on Friday night Nov. 12th.

Mon. Nov. 8th I started
for Russellville, at 4 oclock in
the morning, to accompany
the sisters who had to attend
Court — Went in our Carriage
in company with E. Benjamin,
Eleazar, E. Sister Malinda Bu-
channan, & Wm Lagier. The
Court decided in our favor a-
gainst BOON, & we all returned
home (about 20 in number) in
4 carriages, Wed. evening Nov. 10th

Monday Dec. 13th 1830.
E. Benjamin started in our
Carriage for Frankfort to
attend the Legislature on ac=
count of that wicked law
passed against the believers
of this State in the year 1828:
And Wm Lagier for company:
Staid at Frankfort about 20
days, & at P. Hill about 10
days, & 13 days travelling:
And returned to South
Union, safe home, Monday
January 24th 1831.

Transcription of Document 5

Excerpts from the Molly Goodrich Journal, 1805–1831

Excerpt A

Journal

Tuesday Jan: 1st, 1805: E. John Meacham, Benjamin S. Young, & Issachar Bates, took their journey from N. Lebanon to the Western Country.—

They arrived at Lexington, State of Kentucky, Wednesday March 11th—at Cincinnati, State of Ohio, Tues. March 19th. And the week following and onward, the people near Lebanon in the Miami Country believe and receive the Gospel.

Excerpt B

there believe & receive the Gospel.—Benjamin & other Brethren returned to Miami. Fri. August 2d.

Mon. June 29th E. David, Solomon King & Daniel Moseley, arrived at Miami. They left N.L. Mon. June 1st.

Thu. August 8th Benjamin Malcham & Richard set out for Kentucky by Eagle C. The 3d week in August the people at Shawanoe Run in Mercer County, Ky. believe & receive the Gospel; and the week following those in Shelby.

Benjamin returned to Miami Thu. Sept. 19th. Richard & Malcham having returned separately before.

Thu. Sept. 26th Issachar set out for N.L. At night the wicked burnt down the Believers Stand. Issachar returned to Miami Tue. Dec. 12th.

Wed. Oct. 9th E. John and Benjamin set out for Eagle C. and

Excerpt C

and Kentucky.—Their horses' ears & tails cut off near Danville, Mon. Nov. 11th at night.—B. W. Stone the preacher at Cane Ridge, shut his door against them, Mon. Nov. 25th.—Some receive the Gospel in Mason, the last week in November.—They returned to Miami, Thu. Dec. 5th.

Mon. Dec. 9th Daniel, Benjamin & Malcham set out for Beulah. Returned. Wed. 11th & in the night Malcham's house beset & windows broke.

Mon. Dec. 30th Benjamin, Issachar & Richard set out for Eagle C. & Kentucky.—The first week in Feb. 1806. the people at Paint Lick in Garrard Co. Ky. obey the Gospel, having believed nearly a year. The Brethren returned to Turtle Creek Wed. March 12th 1806.

Wed. March 26th 1806. Benjamin, Issachar & Richard set out for Beulah.—The people there obey the Gospel having believed about a year.—Brethren returned Tues. May 4th.

Excerpt D

Wed. July 18th 1810. Issachar, & John Rankin set out for Bussero & Kentucky. Issachar returned with Joseph, March 20th 1811.

Tues. August 14th I set out for Kentucky, in company with Lucy Bacon, Malcham, Calvin, Polly Thomas & Rosanna Shields—returned (with Constant) Tues. Sept 3d.

Fri. August 24th Eliab & William (with Matthew H.) returned from Kentucky.

Mon. August 27th. This day an extraordinary Mob consisting of upwards of 600 armed men, came against the Believers in order to force them to renounce their faith or quit the country.

Thu. Sept 13th Eliab, William & Constant start for N. Lebanon. At the same time, Archabald, Benjamin & Calvin set out for Bussero, & go & return through wilderness, & arrive again Tues. Dec. 4th.

Excerpt E

Tues. Sept 9. 1818. F. Davis, M. Ruth, E. Solomon, & E. Hortensia at South Union and again for home on Thur. Sept. 17.

Mon. Jan. 4. 1819. John Meigs starts for West Union to assist for a while in the Deacon's line.—and returned.

Thur. Feb. 11. 1819. Joseph Allen starts for U. Village on his return to the East.

Thur. June 17. 1819. The President James Monroe, and Gen'l Andrew Jackson, & suits dined at South Union.

Wed. June 30. 1819. The Believers at South Union abolished slavery.

Tues. Oct. 5. 1819. I set out for Union Village in company with John McComb & Gaty Rubart.—Returned. Nov. 7.

Sun. Jany. 2d. 1820. E. Issachar & Wm. Davis arrived from West Union.—Returned. Jany. 13.

Excerpt F

Mon. Sept. 17th. at U. Village, met a company of friends from South Union, good Sister Mercy, & Maggie Naylor, Lefre McComb, & Benj. Goodhope. Stay at U. Vil. 6 days.

Monday Sept. 24th our whole South Union company in 3 carriages, left Union Village & arrive at P. Hill, Thu. Sept. 27th.

Stay at P. Hill 5 days.

Wed. October 3d. Our whole company, 9 in number, left P. Hill, & all arrived home at South Union in good health, good union, & fine spirits, on Sunday, p.m. Oct. 7th & Received a kind welcome home.

Thus ended our long journey of 1155 miles & the long anticipated visit to my native country & our gospel friends in the East. Gone 5 months, 15 days.

South Union, Thu. May 22d. 1828. E. Benjamin, starts for P. Hill, by particular request, on account of the late law paper against the believers of this State by the Legislature last winter, & to assist Eleazar in publishing a remonstrance. E. Benjamin went in a Dearborn & took Robinson Eads for company & returned home, Sunday, June 22d. & brought along the New publication called *"Investigator."*

Thur. August 21st E. Benjamin set out with Eli McLean for Nashville, & Franklin, in Tennesse, to settle the last business of Willie W. Jones with his agent John H. Eaton— & returned. Thur. Aug. 28.

Excerpt G

Friday August 6th 1830. Eleazar arrived here from P. Hill to know how a suit brought against the believers by John Boon, would be coming on. He returned for P. Hill & U. Village in company with Francis Whyte, Wed. Aug 25th.

Note. E. Benjamin, & Eleazar, & 6 or 10 brethren more, and 8 sisters, attended Court at Russellville, Tues. Aug. 10th. The court decided that the case should be continued to the next November term, & so all the brethren & sisters returned home (in 4 carriages) on Wed. evening August 11th.

Tues. Oct. 12th 1830. & the 3 following days, the *Church Covenant* at South Union signed.—Frid. Oct. 15th Francis and Eleazar return from Union Village & P. Hill: And, Sunday, Oct. 17. Francis spoke beautifully in public, as well as in private meetings— but behold! within 18 hours after this, he closed his eyes in peace, & departed this life into the *world* of spirits, the *"realms up above"*—a world far better than this!—And, Eleazar after [words obscured] attending the court at

Excerpt H

at Russellville in company with E. Benjamin, & the rest & paying all his visits at South Union, departed from Union Village in the Mail Stage, and starts from the Office on Friday night Nov. 12th.

Mon. Nov. 8th I started for Russellville, at 4 oclock in the morning, to accompany the sisters who had to attend Court—Went in our Carriage in company with E. Benjamin, Eleazar, E. Sister Malinda, Bushannan, & Wm. Lagier. The Court decided in our favor against Boon, & we all returned home (about 20 in number) in 4 carriages, Wed. evening Nov. 10th.

Monday, Dec. 13th 1830. E. Benjamin started in our Carriage for Frankfort to attend the Legislature on account of that wicked law paper against the believers of this state in the year 1828. and Wm. Lagier for company: Staid at Frankfort about 20 days; & at P. Hill about 10 days, & 13 days travelling: And returned to South Union, safe home, Monday January 24th 1831.

Historical Background

In the early 19th century the United Society of Believers in Christ's Second Coming, the people called Shakers, numbered some 6,000 souls living primarily in New York, New England, Ohio, and Kentucky. Today only a handful of Shakers remain, their once vital community nearly extinct. Little is remembered of their religious convictions and practices. When recalled at all, it is usually for their simple way of life and the practical beauty of their furniture.

There is far more to the United Society of Believers, however, than the popular images of a quaint and peaceful 19th century religious movement. The Shakers propagated a "new gospel" of communal life and celibacy that provoked opposition and persecution wherever they went. Aggressive missionaries, they pushed westward, successfully expanding the "one true church" along the frontier. The Shaker story is a memorable chapter in our history, providing us with insights into the struggles of minority religious groups for religious liberty in America.

The excerpts from Molly Goodrich's journal (document 5) chronicle the adversity and persecution suffered by the Shakers during the time of their greatest expansion, 1805–1831. The small pages (actual size) of terse, straightforward entries suggest the sparse simplicity of Shaker life. Taken together, these pages reveal the courage and determination of the Believers as they worked to build their communities and spread their gospel.

History and Theology of the Shakers

The journal is a private and brief record of key events, not an attempt to discuss Shaker beliefs or practices. Understanding the entries, therefore, requires some knowledge of the faith's origins.

The United Society of Believers in Christ's Second Coming began in the mid-18th century as an offshoot of an English Quaker group led by James and Ann Wardley. Followers of the Wardleys, "wrestling in soul to be freed from the power of sin and a worldly life," often trembled and writhed during worship, a practice that led others to call them "Shakers."

The founder of Shakerism was an Englishwoman, Ann Lee Stanley (1736–1784), who had joined the Wardleys in 1758. While in prison for breaking the Sabbath by dancing and shouting, Ann Lee had revelations that the second coming of Christ would be in the form of a woman and she was that woman.

In 1774 Ann Lee, called "Mother Ann" by her followers, was directed by a revelation to go with a small group to America. The first Shaker Society in New Lebanon, New York, became the central church of "the one true church." Religious revivals in America during this period created an opening for new teachings. Soon there were Shaker communities in New York, Massachusetts, and Connecticut.

Like other perfectionist groups of the time, the Shakers believed themselves to be the vanguard of the millennium, the thousand-year rule of Christ on earth. They separated themselves from the world and organized communal societies in which all property was made "a consecrated whole."

In Shaker theology, Jesus represents the male manifestation of Christ and Mother Ann the female manifestation. Mother Ann taught that with the Second Coming, Believers must now pattern their lives after the Kingdom of God. This meant that marriage must be abandoned (since the sin of Adam was in sexual impurity) and celibacy adopted as the way of life for the dawn of God's rule. A celibate life would help to raise men and women from animal to spiritual states. The Shakers were convinced that since the end was near there was no longer any need to procreate. The time had come to live a life of absolute purity, giving everything to God for the glory of God's Kingdom.

The Believers Expand Westward

Molly Goodrich's journal records the efforts of the Shakers to spread their new gospel in the early part of the 19th century. Since it is noted that the journal book was given to her in 1812, she made some of the first entries (or copied them from an earlier notebook) at a later date.

The journal begins with three Shaker missionaries, John Meacham, Benjamin Youngs, and Issachar Bates, leaving from New York for western territories on January 1, 1805. With no definite destination in mind, they traveled hundreds of miles seeking a place where Shaker teachings might take root. Unlike most other westward movements, these missions to the West were motivated by religious faith rather than economic opportunity.

Religious revivals in Kentucky and Ohio prior to the arrival of the Shakers created a receptive climate for the new gospel of Mother Ann. Reports of revival meetings where people fell into trancelike states and jerked their head and body led the Shaker missionaries to anticipate fertile soil for Shaker practices. Their hopes were fulfilled when a number of the leaders of this revival, including prominent New Light Presbyterian ministers, were won to the Shaker cause, often bringing members of their congregation with them into the fold.

The missionaries met with considerable success. The western headquarters for the church was established at Union Village, Ohio. The first western covenant, an agreement to dedicate all property to the church and to live in a communal society, was signed in 1810 by 15 brethren and 18 sisters. From there the missionaries and their new converts went out into the wilds of Kentucky, Indiana, and Illinois preaching their gospel. By 1823 there were some 1,700 Shakers in the West.

The Shaker message appealed to many because it offered a new way of life to those already touched by the great awakenings of the revival movement. Shakers went beyond the revivalists' preaching of salvation and the coming of Christ. For them, Christ had already come again. A new order had been established, the "one true church" that separated Believers from the corruption of the world in anticipation of God's rule on earth. The purity and simplicity of the Shaker communal life and the enthusiasm and drama of Shaker worship was a potent combination to those seeking to live according to God's will in the "last days." People joined to become part of an intercessory remnant that would call all men and women to blessedness.

Persecution of the Shakers

As the entries in the journal testify, the Believers also met with great opposition everywhere they went. The belief that Christ had come, the vow of celibacy, and the practice of holding all property in common were aspects of Shakerism that proved particularly offensive to the various Christian groups. Other Shaker beliefs, notably their opposition to slavery and their refusal to bear arms, also inspired opposition in the West.

False stories were spread about Shakers claiming, among other things, that they castrated their males, beat their children, and incited Indians to fight the government. These rumors helped to whip up fear and animosity toward the Shakers. The journal records the burning of a Shaker stand (place of worship), the mutilation of horses, and mob attacks—all common actions taken against the Believers by their neighbors.

The greatest show of force noted by Molly Goodrich was the mob of 600 armed men who "came against the Believers in order to force them to renounce their faith or quit the country." That event took place at Union Village on August 27, 1810. The mob marched on the Shaker community to force the release of children they believed were held against their wishes and to demand that the Shakers give up their beliefs and practices. The Believers replied that the U.S. Constitution protected their right to worship as they pleased, and that the children were there with the consent of their fathers. Leaders of the mob questioned the children and searched for others believed to be imprisoned and abused. Finding nothing, the crowd reluctantly withdrew.

The presence of children in Shaker communities was a frequent source of opposition to the Society of Believers. Some of these children entered the community with one parent, usually the father, while the other parent remained unconverted. Though it was against the tenets of Shaker faith to receive children against the will of either parent, such cases did occur.

A number of states with strong Shaker communities, including Ohio in 1811 and New York in 1818, passed laws aimed at restricting the rights of parents who joined the Shakers. The New York law, for example, gave the state the right to award custody of the child to the parent who was not a Believer. Hearing about the act in 1817, Thomas Jefferson was moved to write to Albert Gallatin:

> Three of our papers have presented us the copy of an act of the legislature of New York, which, if it has really passed, will carry us back to the times of darkest bigotry and barbarism, to find a parallel. Its purport is, that all those who shall hereafter join in communion with the religious sect of Shaking Quakers, shall be deemed civilly dead, their marriages dissolved, and all their children and property taken out of their hands (Papers of Thomas Jefferson).

Property disputes were another source of trouble for the Shakers wherever they settled. Those who left the Believers sometimes demanded the return of property given to the order when they joined. Some state legislatures attempted to make it easier to bring suit against the Shakers. The "wicked law" of 1828 (twice mentioned in the journal) was a Kentucky law making it possible to file suit against the Shaker communities without designating individuals or serving any subpoena other than one attached to a meeting house door.

Fortunately for the Shakers, suits brought against them for recovery of property (such as the suit of John Boon mentioned in the Goodrich journal) were unsuccessful. The courts upheld the Shaker covenant as a binding contract. In 1834, for example, former Shakers in Pleasant Hill, Kentucky, sued for the return of their property, claiming, among other charges, that the use of the property was for "superstitious" purposes. Rejecting the claim, the state court wrote:

> [W]e have no established religion . . . by our constitution, all religions are viewed as equally orthodox. . . . It is neither for the legislature nor the judiciary in this state, to discriminate and say, what is a pious and what a superstitious use (Andrews 1953).

Despite opposition and some persecution, the principles of religious liberty in the U.S. Constitution and in state constitutions did offer protection to the Shakers. In another property case, this one in New Hampshire, the court admitted the merits of Shaker life. More significantly, the court held that "their faith" must be equally protected by the Constitution:

No one can see the improvements made in husbandry and manufactures by this sect, and at the same time believe the existence of the sect to be against the policy of the law. Whatever we may think of their faith, their works are good, and charity bids us think well of the tree when the fruits are salutary. We cannot try the question which religion, theirs or ours, is the better one. . . . Theirs is equally under the protection of the law, as ours. . . . There certainly are some reasons for saying that the religion of this sect of Christians bears a greater resemblance to that of the primitive church than ours does (Andrews 1953).

The Shakers Today

At the time of Molly Goodrich's last journal entry in 1831 the Shakers had 19 communities from Kentucky to Maine and some 6,000 members. In the latter 19th century, the number of members rapidly declined and the communities were abandoned one by one. Today there are nine members at the Shaker community in Sabbathday Lake, Maine, and two members at the Shaker community in Canterbury, New Hampshire.

References
Andrews, Edward O. (1953). *The People Called Shakers: A Search for the Perfect Society*. New York: Dover Publications.
Papers of Thomas Jefferson. Washington, D.C.: Library of Congress.

Suggestions for Using the Document

Discussion Questions

1. After a brief introduction to Shaker history and theology, distribute the journal excerpts and ask students to read the journal entries aloud. Note that the facsimiles represent the actual size of the journal.
2. What is a journal? Does anyone in the class keep a journal or diary? If so, has anyone else read your journal? Why are journals especially rich sources for understanding the events of history?
3. Journals or diaries are often very personal documents. What do we learn about Molly Goodrich from reading her journal? Why do you think she kept this journal?
4. What can be learned about Shaker beliefs and practices from the language and writing style in the journal?
5. Shakers were a self-effacing people who practiced a very simple way of life. Is there evidence of this in the journal?

6. The Shakers attempted to form a utopian society based on communistic principles. Discuss the challenges of creating an ideal society. What are some other examples of utopian movements in U.S. history?
7. How did their religious faith enable the Shakers to endure their hardships?
8. What about the Shakers caused others to fear them? Do you think these fears were justified?
9. Compare the experiences of the Shakers with those of new religious groups in America today. Does the First Amendment protect all religious practices? Are there limits to "free exercise" of religion?
10. Some parents have hired deprogrammers in an attempt to remove their children from religious groups they find objectionable. Is deprogramming constitutional?
11. Does the state have the right to intervene in the practice of religion in order to protect the lives of the adherents?

Extension Activity

Ask students to think of themselves as historians investigating early 19th century America. Divide the class into small groups and ask them to consider the following questions while closely examining the journal entries:

a. Do you think Molly Goodrich gives an accurate account of the events she describes? Why or why not?
b. How much should the historian trust the account of someone who is involved in the events reported?
c. What are some other ways to verify the incidents mentioned in the journal?
d. Is it possible to get a clear and unbiased picture of what actually happened?
e. What other developments in early 19th century America may have contributed to resentment of the Shakers for their pacifist and abolitionist views?
f. Does the journal suggest the motives for Shaker expansion westward? Compare Shaker reasons for going West to the motivations of others during the same period.

Research Topics

1. Examine the prominent leadership role of women in a number of other important religious movements in American history (for example, Christian Science, Theosophical Society).
2. Identify and discuss some other utopian experiments in American history.
3. What factors caused the Shaker membership to decline?
4. Explore the tensions created by new religious movements in contemporary America.

Additional Resources

Andrews, Edward D. (1953). *The People Called Shakers: A Search for the Perfect Society*. New York: Dover Publications, Inc. The best book about the history of the Shakers.

The Bill of Rights in Action: Freedom of Religion. (1969). Pasadena, Calif.: Barr Films. A 21-minute film about a blood transfusion case that explores the tensions between some religious practices and the interests of the state to protect the health and safety of its citizens.

Bromley, David G., and James T. Richardson, eds. (1984). *The Brainwashing-Deprogramming Controversy: Sociological, Psychological, Legal and Historical Perspectives* (Studies in Religion and Society: Vol. 5). Lewiston, N.Y.: Edwin Mellen Press. A collection of articles that explores First Amendment questions involving new religious movements.

Sasson, Diane. (1983). *Shaker Spiritual Narrative*. Knoxville: University of Tennessee Press. An excellent study of Shaker autobiographies in the 19th century.

For more information about the Shakers today, Shaker historical sites, and Shaker documents, write to:

The Shaker Library at Sabbathday Lake, Maine
United Society of Shakers
RR #1, Box 640
Poland Spring, Maine 04274

Shaker Village, Inc.
288 Shaker Road
Canterbury, New Hampshire, 03224

4

The Beginnings of Nativism in America

An Anti-Catholic petition from New York nativists to the U.S. Congress, 1837

ocument 6

Anti-Catholic petition from New York nativists to the U.S. Congress, 1837

rce: National Archives, Washington, D.C.

To the Honorable the Senate and House of Representatives of the United States, in Congress Assembled:

The Memorial of your petitioners humbly sheweth, that seldom has a nation arisen, prospered, declined and fallen, without feeling, in the time of their prosperity and begun decline, an ominous confidence in the strength of their institutions, and a fatal disregard of that which ultimately effected their ruin. This should teach us caution.

Experience has proved the weakness of all human institutions under the attacks of corrupt principles, and has made the fact evident that the material of their strength lies in the intelligence, sound principles, and good morals of the people. This experience shows the necessity of vigilance, and especially of a vigilant eye on all principles and measures, which, though they be at present feebly supported, yet when they acquire strength, are sufficient to subvert the liberties of the State.

Our equal right of suffrage, which is the great excellence of our political institutions, is, by abuse and intrigue on the one hand, and unsuspecting confidence on the other, the chief avenue of danger: and this has not escaped the notice of eagle-eyed despotism. The easy access of foreigners to the elective franchise in the United States, by the present laws of naturalization, and of foreigners of doubtful morals and hostile political principles, is a source of danger to our civil and religious liberties, to which your Memorialists would humbly and earnestly invite the speedy attention of Congress.

Equal right of suffrage is the right of the majority to rule; but our constitution did not contemplate a majority hostile to its principles. And by the very fact of naturalization laws, our nation says—We have principles, privileges and institutions which we cherish, and will maintain, and in opposition to which, no foreigner shall have a right of suffrage with us. If we cherish civil and religious liberties and esteem them above all price, we have a right to defend them from foreign invasion; whether it approach by open warfare, or insidiously by obtaining the privilege of citizenship. Since naturalization laws have been judged necessary, let them be adequate for our defence. Our country has happily been the asylum of the poor and oppressed of other nations; let it still be worthy of the name, and not yield to a despotism which none may court to enjoy. Let us see that those admitted from the lap of tyranny to the right of suffrage with us be indeed the friends of our cherished liberties.

Your Memorialists view with deep concern the great influx of Roman Catholics into this country from the various nations of Europe, and their admission to citizenship while they retain their principles, as eminently threatening our civil and religious liberties. Dr. Robertson in his history of Scotland, says of Popery that it "prepares and breaks the mind for political servitude"—that it is 'a system of superstition which is the firmest foundation of civil tyranny"—"a religion, whose very spirit as well as practice is persecuting, sanguinary and encroaching."

Against Roman Catholics, as men, we have no hostility. Against their religion, in its religious character, we ask no legislation, offensive or defensive; we leave it to be combatted by the appropriate weapons of education and religious institutions; but against political principles interwoven with their religion, we do ask legislative defence. This distinction must be made if we would not be the dupes and victims of foreign intrigue. Our constitution happily allows the free toleration of all religions; it is for this toleration that we plead against a religion which refuses it. Does our constitution, by allowing the toleration of all religions, contemplate the toleration of a politically intolerant religion? the toleration of political principles subversive of our free institutions, merely because interwoven with a religious creed? Are political principles subversive of our free institutions less dangerous, or less the subjects of constitutional condemnation, because they are part of a religious system? Does our constitution intend to tolerate a religion, which would erect a church establishment subjecting the civil authorities, and our civil and religious liberties, to its religious and despotic control? Does it allow the mere name of religion to sanctify such political principles subversive of its very spirit and intention? Our constitution is not suicidal.

Your Memorialists, unwilling to encroach further on your patience, earnestly petition your honorable body to inquire whether the principles of Roman Catholics, as held at present as well as formerly, are not political and hostile to civil and religious liberty; and whether their religion is not essentially political, requiring the union of Church and State, and the subjection of the latter to the former: and whether it does not require allegiance to the Pope of Rome, holding the obligation to obey him, as paramount to all other authority, and his subjects not bound even by an oath, when he requires the breach of it for the sake of his religion? And whether it does not justify, and imperiously require, legislative defence against this influence in our government; and further, whether there be not a plan in operation, powerful and dangerous, under the management of the Leopold Foundation, for the subversion of our civil and religious liberties, to be effected by the emigration of Roman Catholics from Europe, and by their admission to the right of suffrage with us in our political institutions; and further, whether any amendment of the laws of naturalization can more fully secure our free institutions, our liberties, civil and religious, against the danger of subversion by foreign influence, and despotic tyrannical principles, even under the cloak of religion. All which is respectfully submitted.

NOVEMBER, 1837.

Document 6 (continued)

NAMES.	RESIDENCE.
James P. Miller	Argyle Washington Co. N.Y.
John Stott	Fort-Edward &c.
John Reid	Argyle
John Bishop	Argyle
James Robertson	Greenwich
... McEachron	Argyle
Samuel Dobbin	Greenwich
John Henry	"
Gilbert Robertson	Argyle
Arch. McNeil	Argyle
John Bain	
John Knickerbocker	Argyle
George Boyd	Argyle
John M. Reid	Greenwich
Thomas Beveridge	Argyle
Wm Boyd	Argyle
George Liddrum	Argyle
Robert G. Hall	Argyle
Cornelius ch.	

Historical Background

The great influx of Irish Catholic and other immigrants into the United States in the early 19th century sparked a vicious outbreak of nativism. Petitions from the northeast states, including one in 1837 from 97 electors in Washington County, New York (document 6), were sent to Congress demanding that laws be passed to keep the franchise from the new arrivals.

Fear of "foreign" influence, particularly Roman Catholic, was not a new phenomenon in 1837. The Protestants who settled the eastern seaboard of North America may have differed in significant ways, but they were united in their opposition to the Church of Rome. By the time of the American Revolution, Guy Fawkes Day, also called "Pope Day," was still celebrated in Massachusetts and other colonies by burning the pope in effigy. Even after the adoption of the Constitution, Roman Catholics could not hold public office in most states until 1806.

Despite this widespread hostility, the Roman Catholic population in the United States grew steadily from some 30,000 in 1784 to more than 300,000 by 1820. The growing numbers of Catholic and other immigrants stirred fears in America that the "foreign-born" would bring antidemocratic, "absolutist" ideas from Europe. Allegiance to the Pope, in particular, was seen by many as allegiance to a foreign political power bent on subverting America's free institutions. John Adams reflected the view of many in the new nation when he wrote in 1821 that "a free government and the Roman Catholic religion can never exist together in any nation or Country" (Leonard and Parment 1971).

The Challenges of Immigration

By November 1837, anti-Catholic sentiment had coalesced into a powerful nativist movement. The petition reproduced here states directly and concisely the bitter anti-Catholic sentiments that would mark subsequent nativist movements well into the 20th century. Catholic immigration was seen as a "foreign invasion," a plot to establish "despotic" control over the United States. Underneath this hysteria was the nativists' fear that a Catholic loyal to the Pope in Rome could not be in real sympathy with the American system and must, therefore, be a danger to that system.

Antipathy toward Catholicism was fueled by the waves of immigration between the 1820s and 1850s. A large measure of the hostility and fear was directed at the Irish Catholics entering the country through New York. Anti-Catholicism was joined to social, political, and economic issues as the Irish Catholics made their presence felt in America. Some Americans suspected that other countries were dumping their poor in the United States, and they blamed the uneducated, unskilled immigrants for a wide range of social ills, such as poverty, crime, and disease. Many working men saw the new arrivals as competition for scarce jobs and the cause of low wages, rising rents, and worsening labor conditions. Government, too, resented the new Americans. In 1930, New York City complained that its social services were overwhelmed by the "foreign element."

Confronted by these challenging conditions and deep-seated prejudices, the Irish Catholics of New York looked to the Roman Catholic Church as a haven of support in the new world. Charitable and educational efforts of the Church were instrumental in helping immigrants adjust to a confusing and often hostile environment. Ironically, the efforts of the Church to help the immigrants were cited by the nativists as further evidence of foreign "clannishness" and refusal to accept American values and customs.

Conspiracy Theories and Hate Campaigns

The harsh accusations of the petition go beyond expressing anti-Catholic attitudes to suggest a conspiracy by the Roman Catholic Church against the United States. Much of the petitioners' language might well have been lifted from the writings of Samuel F. B. Morse, inventor of the telegraph and the leading nativist of the 1830s and 1840s. The publication in 1834 of Morse's *The Foreign Conspiracy Against the Liberties of the United States* did much to convince many Americans that Rome was using illiterate immigrants as pawns in a plot to unify church and state and thus destroy American liberties.

The "evidence" of a conspiracy offered by Morse (and mentioned in the petition) was the existence of the Leopold Foundation, a Catholic organization intended to aid church expansion in America. Morse interpreted the missionizing efforts of the Catholic Church as the Catholic hierarchy's master plan to gain control of American society.

Morse's sentiments were echoed by the prominent Protestant clergyman Lyman Beecher. In his famous statement *A Plea for the West*, Beecher warned that the "Catholics and infidels" were fast gaining ground in the American West. He exhorted Americans to save the West for Protestantism and liberty by resisting the "union of church and state" advocated by the Catholics.

Morse and Beecher saw the Catholic "menace" as an opportunity to reawaken a sense of Protestant unity and reestablish the mission of building a "Christian America." They and other nativist leaders viewed the Protestant faith as the basis for American ideals and essential to the survival of American institutions.

The efforts to kindle a Protestant mission in America inspired widespread social reform movements in the first half of the 19th century.

Unfortunately, the anti-Catholic propaganda that accompanied some of the reform efforts also aroused hatred and stirred fears, particularly in the volatile urban centers where tensions between natives and immigrants were most acute. In 1834, for example, after a series of inflammatory speeches in Boston churches by Beecher, a mob burned the Ursuline Convent School. Other riots would follow in the next two decades, resulting in the loss of life and the destruction of Catholic churches.

In 1836, one of the vilest and most popular pieces of anti-Catholic literature, *The Awful Disclosures of the Hotel Dieu Nunnery of Montreal* by Maria Monk, was published in New York. Monk claimed that as a novice in a convent she witnessed every manner of evil imaginable. According to her very explicit account, the convent was a place of sexual sin and the murder of babies by priests and nuns. Even after the book was exposed as the complete fabrication of a mentally disturbed girl, it continued to sell briskly. More than 300,000 copies were sold prior to the Civil War.

Nativism in New York Politics

The conspiracy theories and scare literature of the 1830s moved many New Yorkers to organize to block the avenue to Catholic power represented by the Catholic vote. Not only were the immigrant voters part of a "popish plot," they were also seen as uneducated, un-American foreigners completely unqualified to vote. There was the additional fear (not wholly unjustified, given the corrupt state of New York politics in the 1830s) that the new voters would be used by unscrupulous politicians to gain political power.

In 1834 the New York Protestant Association was formed "to spread the knowledge of the gospel truth and to show wherein it is inconsistent with the tenets and dogmas of popery." By 1835 New York nativists had organized politically, running nativists for public office and working to change the naturalization laws. Uniting with the Whigs, the nativists had some limited success in the New York City election of 1837.

Petitions like the one from Washington County poured into Congress during this period, asking for changes in existing naturalization laws to protect America from "foreigners of doubtful morals and hostile political principles." A select committee of the House of Representatives, dominated by nativists, endorsed legislation in 1838 that would have greatly extended the probationary period for naturalization. Though this bill did not pass the full House, the stage was set for future nativist campaigns by the Native American party of the 1840s and the Know-Nothing movement of the 1850s.

The Catholic Response

The exaggerated and ugly nativist attacks on the Roman Catholic Church were rooted in the centuries-old conflict between Protestantism and Catholicism in Europe. Each side distrusted the other as the enemy of the true church, and each side was deeply suspicious of the other's political motives.

When Samuel Morse traveled to Europe in the early 1830s, he found a very conservative Catholic Church often allied with reactionary political forces. Though Morse was sadly mistaken about papal "conspiracies," he correctly understood the traditional Catholic view that the state should recognize the Catholic Church as the religion of the commonwealth. Much like the Puritan founders of Massachusetts, conservative Catholics believed that the state and the church have separate areas of responsibility, but they are required by divine law to work cooperatively in a society wholly dependent on God.

What Morse refused to understand or appreciate was that many Catholics in America had long supported the American experiment in religious liberty. Early Maryland, a colony founded as a refuge for English Catholics, was itself the scene of America's first experiment in religious toleration. John Carroll (1735-1815), the first Roman Catholic bishop in the United States, was a strong defender of freedom of conscience and a sensitive interpreter to Rome of the American situation.

As their numbers grew, Catholics in the United States generally accepted the American independence of church and state. Paulist Father Edward Brady, writing at the end of the 19th century, expressed the views of many American Catholics when he wrote that, should the Catholic Church ever be in the majority, "she would not touch a single stone in the noble fabric of our constitution—nay, she would safeguard to the utmost of her power our free institutions, and teach her children to be willing at any moment to die in their defence" (Wilson and Drakeman 1987).

Toleration or Freedom?

Nativist fears of the Catholic "union of Church and State," were no defense of the Religious Liberty clauses of the First Amendment. To the contrary, many nativists were Protestant evangelicals who saw America as a Christian (Protestant) nation. Official disestablishment did not, in their view, seriously challenge the unofficial establishment of Christianity as the American way of life. As Daniel Webster put it: "Christianity—general, tolerant Christianity—Christianity independent of sects and parties—that Christianity to which the sword and the fagot are unknown—general, tolerant Christianity is the law of the land" (Wilson and Drakeman 1987).

The view of Protestantism as a de facto establishment in the United States was echoed, unwittingly perhaps, in the rhetorical question of the Washington County petition: "Does our constitution, by allowing toleration of all religions, contemplate the toleration of a politically intolerant religion?" For the nativists, the question was whether or not Catholics could be tolerated to live in the U.S. at all.

The First Amendment, however, guarantees full freedom of religion to all, not mere toleration by the majority. The arrival of Catholics and Jews in great numbers created a new pluralism in 19th century America and challenged many Americans to confront for the first time the full implications of true religious liberty. For the First Amendment to be taken seriously, freedom of conscience could not be a concession by the majority to the minorities, but an inalienable right beyond the power of the government, or the Protestant majority, to grant or remove.

References

Leonard, Ira M., and Robert D. Parmet. (1971). *American Nativism, 1830-1860.* New York: Van Nostrand Reinhold, p.24.

Wilson, John F., and Donald L. Drakeman. (1987). *Church and State in American History.* Boston: Beacon Press.

Suggestions for Using the Document

Discussion Questions

1. What conditions in the United States of the 1830s contributed to the outbreak of nativism? Why was New York a hotbed of nativist activity?
2. What did the petitioners fear most about the Catholic immigrants?
3. How did the petitioners define religious liberty? Is "toleration" what is guaranteed by the First Amendment?
4. Should the United States exclude immigrants on the basis of religious or political belief?
5. Discuss nativist attitudes in America today.

Extension Activities

1. Divide the class into research groups. Assign each group one of the major ethnic groups now entering the United States in significant numbers (e.g., Hispanics, Asians). How do the current immigration laws affect these new arrivals? What, if any, religious problems do these groups encounter in the United States? What has the reception been for each of these groups?
2. Ask students to discuss with parents and grandparents how and when their ancestors came to America. Did they encounter nativist attitudes?

Research Topics

1. Examine the political climate of New York in the 1830s
2. What was the Leopold Foundation?
3. Explore the roots of anti-Catholicism in colonial America.
4. What were the views of the first American Roman Catholic bishop, John Carroll, concerning religious liberty?

Additional Resources

Billington, Ray Allen. (1964). *The Protestant Crusade, 1800–1860: A Study of the Origins of American Nativism.* Chicago: Quadrangle.

Higham, John. (1975). *Strangers in the Land: Patterns of American Nativism, 1860–1925.* New York: Atheneum.

5

Anti-Semitism in America

Senator Lazarus Powell's resolution
condemning General Order
No. 11, January 5, 1863, and
Captain Philip Trounstine's resignation
from the U.S. Army, March 3, 1863

cument 7

tor Lazarus Powell's resolution condemning General Order No. 11, January 5, 1863

ce: National Archives, Washington, D.C.

37 Cong.
3 Sess.

Resolution
by Mr Powell in
relation to an order
issued by Major Genl.
U. S. Grant, expelling
Jews from the depart-
ment of which he
is in Command &c.

1863 Jany. 5. Submitted.
" Jany 9. Resumed. ~~Clerk~~
~~take for indefinitely~~
~~Powell for &c~~ Hale to
lie on table - Powell for &c
yeas-30 Nays 7 —

Whereas Maj. Gen. U. S. Grant of the
Army of the United States on the 17th day
of December 1862 issued the following
General order

Document 7 (continued)

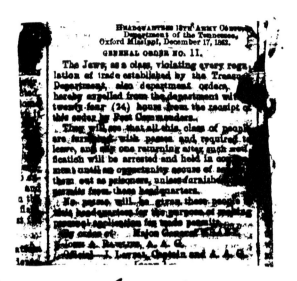

and whereas by virtue of said order the Jews as a class — who claim to be loyal citizens of the United States, have been expelled from the city of Paducah Kentucky — and have been driven from their business and homes by the military authority, without any specific charges having been made against them, or any opportunity given them to meet the vague and general charges set forth in said order; therefore

cument 7 (continued)

Resolved, By the senate of the United
states that the said order of maj. Gen.
grant, expelling the jews as a class
from the department, of which he is in
command is condemned, as illegal, ~~tyranical~~
tyronical, cruel and unjust; And the
resident is requested to countermand the same,

Transcription of Document 7

Senator Lazarus Powell's resolution condemning General Order No. 11, January 5, 1863

37 Cong. 3 Sess.}

Resolution by Mr. Powell in relation to an order issued by Major Genl. U.S. Grant, expelling Jews from the department of which he is in command etc.

> 1863 Jany. 5. Submitted.
> "—Jany. 9.—Resumed—
> Hale to *lie on table*—Powell for Y & N
> yeas-30 nays7—

Whereas Maj. Gen. U.S. Grant of the Army of the United States on the 17th day of December 1862 issued the following general order

Headquarters 13th Army Corps
Department of the Tennessee,
Oxford Mississippi, December 17, 1862

GENERAL ORDER NO. 11.

The Jews, as a class, violating every regulation of trade established by the Treasury Department, also department orders, are hereby expelled from the department within twenty-four (24) hours from the receipt of this order by Post Commanders.

They will see that all this class of people are furnished with passes and required to leave, and any one returning after such notification will be arrested and held in confinement until an opportunity occurs of sending them out as prisoners, unless furnished with permits from these headquarters.

No passes will be given these people to visit headquarters for the purpose of making personal application for trade permits.

By order of Major General GRANT
John A. Rawlins, A. A. G.
Official—J. Lovell, Captain and A. A. G.

and whereas by virtue of said order the Jews as a class—who claim to be loyal citizens of the United States—have been expelled from the city of Paducah Kentucky—and have been driven from their business and homes by the military authority, without any specific charges having been made against them, or any opportunity given them to meet the vague and general charges set forth in said order: Therefore Resolved. By the senate of the United States that the said order of Maj. Gen. Grant, expelling the Jews as a class from the department, of which he is in command is condemned, as illegal, tyranical, cruel and unjust; and the President is requested to countermand the same.

cument 8

ain Philip Trounstine's resignation from the U.S. Army, March 3, 1863
ce: National Archives, Washington, D.C.

Head Quarters Co "B" 5th Reg. O.V.C.
4th Division 16th Army Corps
Moscow Tennessee March 3rd 1863

Major C. S. Hayes
Comdg 5th Rg. OVC.

Majors!
I respectfully
address, you, on the subject of tendering you. with
this, my resignation of The commission I now
hold, as Captain of Company "B" 5th Regt.
Ohio Volunteer Cavalry.—
The reasons for offering
the above, are few, and I shall Therefore try
to be as concise as possible in presenting them
to your consideration.—

Document 8 (continued)

You are perhaps
well aware of my having been either fortunately
or unfortunately born of Jewish parents; my
futurity must of course decide which; you will
therefore bear with me, Major, when I say that so
alone; my feelings, but the sense of Religious
duty, I owe to the religion of my forefathers,
were both deeply hurt and wounded in consequence of the late order of General Grant
issued December 17th 1862, in which all persons
of collatteral religious faith with my own,
were ordered to leave this Department —

I do not
wish to argue the question of Order No. 11 being
either right or wrong, nor would I, if even I
dared to, But I cannot help feeling, that as
I owe filial affection to my parents, Devotion

cument 8 (continued)

to my Religion, and a deep regard for the opinion of my friends and feeling that I can no longer, bear the taunts and malice, of those to whom my religious opinions are known, brought on by the effect that, that order has instilled into their minds, I herewith respectfully tender you my res... immeadiate and unconditional resignation.—

... tify upon honor that I have no property ...u nging to the Government of the United State in my possession.—

I was last paid by paymaster Major Jordan to include August 31st 1862

I have the honor to be, Major, Very Respectfully Your Obedient Servant Philip Frountkine Capt Co "B" 5 Reg. O.S.C.

Transcription of Document 8

Captain Philip Trounstine's resignation from the U.S. Army, March 3, 1863

Head Quarters Co. "B" 5th Reg. O.V.C.
4th Division 16th Army Corps
Moscow Tennessee March 3rd 1863

Major C.S. Hayes
Com 5th Reg. O.V.C.

Major!

I respectfully address, you, on the subject of tendering you with this, my resignation of the commission I now hold, as Captain of Company "B" 5th Regt. Ohio Volunteer Cavalry.—

The reasons for offering the above, are few, and I shall therefore try to be as concise as possible in presenting them to your consideration.—

You are perhaps well aware of my having been, either fortunately or unfortunately born of Jewish parents; my futurity must of course decide which; you will therefore bear with me, Major. when I say that not alone; my feelings, but the sense of Religious duty, I owe to the religion of my Forefathers, were both deeply hurt and wounded in consequence of the late order of General Grant issued December 17th 1862, in which all persons of collatteral religious faith with my own were ordered to leave this Department.—

I do not wish to argue the question of Order No. 11 being either right or wrong, nor would I, if even I dared to, But I cannot help feeling, that as I owe filial affection to my parents, Devotion to my Religion, and a deep regard for the opinion of my friends and feeling that I can no longer, bear the taunts and malice, of those to whom my religious opinions are known, brought on by the effect that, that order has instilled into their minds. I herewith respectfully tender you my immediate and unconditional resignation.—

I certify upon honor that I have no property belonging to the Government of the United States in my possession.—I was last paid by paymaster Major Jordan to include August 31st 1862.

I have the honor to be, Major,
Very Respectfully
Your obedient servant
Philip Trounstine
Capt Co "B." 5th Reg O.V.C.

Historical Background

On December 17, 1862, during the dark days of the Civil War, General Ulysses S. Grant issued General Order No. 11, expelling "Jews as a class" from the Department of Tennessee for trading with the enemy. Nineteen days later, on January 5, an outraged Senator Lazarus Powell of Kentucky submitted a resolution to Congress condemning the order and asking President Lincoln to countermand it (document 7). President Lincoln had already ordered General Halleck to rescind the order, which Halleck did on January 4.

Viewed one way, Grant's order was an isolated incident, a rash act by a Civil War hero during a time of national crisis. Seen in a broader context, however, General Order No. 11 was symbolic of a change in status of American Jews during the Civil War period. The great influx of Jewish immigrants in the mid-19th century made the Jewish community more visible and consequently more vulnerable to attack. As their numbers and influence grew, the small religious minority that had been generally accepted as part of American society became the subject of unflattering stereotypes and the scapegoat for the troubles of the nation. General Grant's order is important, therefore, because of what it tells us about the emergence of anti-Semitism in American history.

The Immediate Cause

The immediate cause for the order was General Grant's anger at the widespread illegal trade with the enemy going on throughout the territories he commanded. Unable to stop the corruption and bribery, Grant lashed out at the Jews, using them as a scapegoat for a growing and increasingly insoluble problem.

In truth, many people on both sides of the conflict, including army officers, were part of the illegal exchange of goods between the North and South. By 1862, Federal troops occupied large areas of Confederate territory, including Louisiana and western Tennessee. Wherever the warring factions touched, particularly in cities like New Orleans and Nashville, a thriving black market was quickly established.

Illegal trading and profiteering was inevitable given the importance of trade between the North and South. The economic interdependence of the two sides had not ended with the outbreak of war. The North continued to need cotton, sugar, rice, and tobacco. And the South desperately needed munitions, medicine, and salt, the latter for curing meat to feed the troops.

The North attempted to outlaw profiteering by promulgating regulations governing trade in occupied territories. But such regulations proved impossible to enforce. Economic pressures forced both sides to wink at deals, even though it was clear that the profits made were aiding the enemy.

General Grant and other army commanders were angered by the fact that the gold paid for cotton went to buy guns and the salt traded went to preserve meat for the South's armies. Many in both governments tolerated huge profits and much corruption in the belief that such trade was militarily and economically necessary. By the end of the war, this belief had been shattered. Many observers, including a committee of Congress, had come to support Grant's contention that illegal trade was demoralizing to both sides, prolonged the war, and cost lives.

A Time of Storm and Stress

General Grant's shocking action against the Jews reflected the widespread bigotry of the times. By the time of the Civil War, nativist xenophobia, which had been directed primarily at Catholics, began to affect Jews as well. With the outbreak of war, Jews became easy targets for charges of disloyalty and scapegoats for the calamities experienced in the North and South. Grant's order contributed significantly to this new climate of anti-Semitism.

By 1864, the attacks had become so pervasive that Simon Wolf, a Jewish leader of the time, wrote a letter of protest to sympathetic newspaper editor William Cullen Bryant:

> The war now raging has developed an insanity of malice that borders upon the darest days of superstition and the Spanish Inquisition. Has the war now raging been inaugurated or fostered by Jews exclusively? Is the late Democratic Party composed entirely of Israelites? Are there no native Americans engaged in rebellion? No Christians running the blockade, or meek followers of Christ within the fold of Tammany?
>
> We have been branded and outraged for four long years, until discretion has ceased to be a virtue. . . . Why, when immediately throughout the Union that a Jew, another Jew blockader, has been caught . . . ? Is it, then, a crime to be born a Jew, which is to be expiated upon the alter of public opinion by a life of suffering and abuse . . . ? I am not now pleading the cause of the Jew, but I am defending the principle that underlies our public institutions, our private worth. Are we to go on in this uncalled-for vituperation and sowing the wind, to reap at last the whirlwind (Belth 1981)?

Many Jews also felt threatened by a revival during the war years of efforts to add a "Christian Amendment" to the U.S. Constitution. From the days of ratification in 1787, many Protestant Americans saw the absence of any reference to God or Christ as a fatal flaw in the Constitution. In the mid-19th century, a number of leading Protestant ministers argued from the pulpit that only by acknowledging the nation's dependence on Christ would the nation enjoy the protection and favor of God.

The suffering and devastation of the Civil War was seen by thousands of religious Americans as God's punishment for the country's omission of Christ from the Constitution. In 1863 leaders from many Protestant churches founded the National Reform Association to fight for rewording the preamble of the Constitution to read: "Recognizing Almighty God as the source of all authority and power in civil government, and acknowledging the Lord Jesus Christ as the governor among the nations, His revealed will as the supreme law of the land, in order to constitute a Christian government. . . ." The National Reform Association attracted powerful supporters and fought for many years to amend the Constitution. Ultimately, however, it was unable to persuade Congress to act on its proposal.

The struggle for a "Christian Amendment" is an illustration of the widespread assumption by many 19th century Americans that the United States was (or should aspire to be) a "Christian nation" or "evangelical empire." There were, to be sure, positive benefits issuing from this vision of America. The many religious awakenings and revivals during this period helped inspire movements to abolish slavery, promote education, and carry out many other social reforms.

At the same time, the fact that many citizens identified America with the Christian mission caused fear and concern among the Jews, particularly in light of the climate of prejudice during the Civil War. The primacy of Christianity was the underlying theme of many speeches, sermons, and even laws of the time. In 1861, for example, Congress passed a law, later repealed after much protest by Jews, requiring that all army chaplains be Christian. A year later, President Lincoln issued an order with "deference to the best sentiment of a Christian people" that all military commanders were to observe Sunday as a day of rest.

All of these factors—immigration, nativism, "Christian nation" sentiments—are part of the backdrop for understanding General Grant's expulsion of the Jews from the territory under his command.

A Misdirected Attack

Grant's terrible mistake was both evil and hypocritical. After all, he was attacking the Jews for activities that a wide variety of people, including many government officials, participated in and supported. Why he singled out the Jews is not entirely clear. Perhaps Jewish traders were a visible and easy target, their expulsion allowing Grant to take at least some symbolic action in the territory he commanded.

As Senator Powell's resolution indicates, the immediate effect of Grant's order in places like Paducah, Kentucky, was to drive Jewish citizens from their homes and businesses. Even those Jews serving in the U.S. army were affected. Captain Philip Trounstine resigned out of loyalty to his Jewish faith and because he could "no longer bear the taunts and malice" (document 8).

Jewish groups strongly protested the order, some calling it an order "worthy of despotic Europe in the dark ages of the world's history" (Papers of Abraham Lincoln). Sadly, many others, including a number of congressmen, rose to Grant's defense. Newspapers inflamed readers with editorials depicting Jews as notorious for making money in illegitimate ways.

President Lincoln rescinded General Grant's order on January 4, 1863. With the offending order already canceled, the Senate declined to condemn Grant's order. Powell's resolution was tabled on January 9 by a vote of 30 to 7. The House tabled a similar motion to censure Grant by a vote of 56 to 53. The president asked his general-in-chief, Henry Halleck, to write to Grant and explain why General Order No. 11 had been revoked. Unfortunately, even while canceling the order (in the mildest of terms), the president raised no objection to the singling out of "Jew peddlers":

> It may be proper to give you some explanation of the revocation of your order expelling all Jews from your department. The President has no objection to your expelling traders and Jew pedlars, which I suppose, was the object of your order, but as it in terms prescribed an entire religious class, some of whom are fighting in our ranks, the President deemed it necessary to revoke it (Papers of Ulysses S. Grant).

A number of years later, Grant apologized to Jews, claiming that the order had been sent "without reflection." But the damage had been done: The publicity surrounding Grant's action contributed to the anti-Semitism of the post–Civil War period. Jews were attacked as a "race" and blamed for every manner of ill faced by the war-torn nation. The stage was set for the widespread social discrimination that Jews have suffered in the United States beginning in the late 19th century.

A Historical Reminder

Mercifully brief as it was, this terrible violation of freedom serves as a valuable historical reminder. First, it illustrates several aspects of a recurring pattern of violations: The incident is the outcome of (1) a justifiable cause for concern, (2) a wider horizon of cultural anxiety triggering a popular backlash, and (3) official insensitivity to the people and issues involved.

Second, it illustrates the consequences of confusion over emotionally charged terms and labels used in public debate. "Christian America," the term behind this case, is understandable if it is used to refer to the historical fact that America's roots are primarily (though

not exclusively) Christian, or the statistical fact that the Christian faith
has nearly always been the majority faith in America. It is neither constitutionally permissible nor historically accurate, however, to use the
term "Christian America," to assert or imply any *official national establishment or semi-establishment* of the Christian faith.

For all of the constitutional guarantees, popular support, and public celebration of religious liberty, and despite the undoubted
superiority of America's record to that of Europe, it is clear that violations of religious liberty are an undeniable fact of the American past
and a continuing menace that requires profound realism and untiring
vigilance in the present.

The American experiment failed once when faced with deep moral
and cultural differences—a failure know as the Civil War. As with the
Civil War itself, all violations of religious liberty are a bone-deep reminder of how difficult it has been to preserve civilization and to better
human life. Those who understand this point are not surprised when
bad times teach us more than good times or when the nation can pass
from triumph to folly without noticing it.

References
Belth, Nathan C. (1981). *Promise to Keep: A Narrative of the American Encounter
    with Anti-Semitism.* New York: Schocken Books.
Papers of Abraham Lincoln. Petition to Lincoln from the American Israelites.
    Washington, D.C.: Library of Congress.
Papers of Ulysses S. Grant. Washington, D.C.: Library of Congress

Suggestions for Using the Documents

Discussion Questions

1. According to Senator Powell, what constitutional rights did
    General Grant ignore? Where are these rights protected in the
    Constitution?
2. What additional provisions of the Constitution, if any, might also
    protect the Jews and other minority religious groups? Do the
    Religious Liberty clauses of the First Amendment apply here?
3. Does the government have the right to suspend constitutional
    rights during wartime? What about the rights of people in
    "occupied territories?" What if the area occupied is part of the
    United States, but in rebellion against the federal government?
4. What were the economic and military conditions that contributed
    to General Grant's anger against the Jews?
5. How does General Order No. 11 compare with actions taken by
    Nazi Germany against the Jews? Discuss the similarities and

differences. Note that the order treats all Jews "as a class" and prohibits any Jew from applying for a trade permit.

6. Discuss Philip Trounstine's reasons for resigning from the army. Do you think he took the right course of action when confronted with General Order No. 11? What would you have done in his place?

Extension Activities

1. Appoint a group of students to be a Senate committee charged with investigating General Order No. 11. Assign other students to play the roles of Grant, Senator Powell, a delegate from the American Israelites, Philip Trounstine, and other witnesses you think appropriate. Ask all of the participants to prepare for a congressional hearing by researching the historical conditions of the period, the constitutional issues involved, and the history of Jews in the United States. Hold the hearing. Conclude with a committee vote on Senator Powell's resolution.

2. Use Senator Powell's resolution and Captain Trounstine's letter to introduce a discussion of anti-Semitism in American life. View *The Little Falls Incident*, a seven-minute film concerning a recent anti-Semitic incident in a New Jersey junior high school. The reactions of the victim, her classmates, the teacher, and principal are useful starting points for a discussion about prejudice in our society. (The film may be ordered from the Anti-Defamation League, 823 United Nations Plaza, New York, N.Y. 10017.)

Research Topics

1. Was General Order No. 11 an issue in the presidential campaign of 1868?
2. Investigate the reactions of the press, the public, Congress, and the military to General Order No. 11.
3. Trace the history of the National Reform Association. Are there contemporary groups in the United States with a similar platform?
4. What are examples of anti-Semitism in the United States today? Compare today's climate with that of 1862.
5. Compare General Order No. 11 with the internment of Japanese Americans by the government during World War II. What are the important similarities and differences?

Additional Resources

Belth, Nathan C. (1981). *A Promise to Keep: A Narrative of the American Encounter with Anti-Semitism.* New York: Schocken Books. A readable and comprehensive history of anti-Semitism in America.

Borden, Morton. (1984). *Jews, Turks, and Infidels. Chapel Hill*: University of North Carolina Press. An excellent study of the Jewish struggle for religious equality in America.

Quinley, Harold E., and Charles Y. Glock. (1983). *Anti-Semitism in America.* New Brunswick: Transaction Books. A good sociological study of anti-Semitism in our own time.

6

The Role of the African American Church

A letter from an African American church
to the Freedmen's Bureau, 1867

Document 9

Letter from an African American Church to the Freedmen's Bureau, April 14, 1867
Source: National Archives, Washington, D.C.

Westmorland County Va near the Hague
, April 14th 1867

Lieut. Henry K. W. Ayres,
Asst S'upt. B. R. F & A. L.
Warsaw, Richmond Co. Va

Lieut:
                We the colored people in
the Dist near the Hague have ac=
=cording to you advice given us last
Fall went on and have succeeded
in erecting one church and school
House, and have another in course
of Erection; and which will be completed
Early in the coming Summer.
            All we want now is a teacher
and Sabbath School Books, and if
we could be furnished with common
school books it would be of the greatest
benefit to us in this our early and
first attempt to educate ourselves.

Document 9 (continued)

We have had to contend against great
prejudices held in the Whites but have
now succeeded so far well.
Our Sabbath School now agoing is
very large. Our building Which is 22×
20 is far insufficient to accommodate
those who seek for light.
    We have appointed Thomas T.
Johnson, our present colored minister
to advise with you and he will call
upon you for help asked in this
letter.

        Henry X Lawson
        Charles X Jones,
        Vincient X Kelly
        Archable X Kelly
        Edmund X Lee
        Peter X Hungerford
        Luke X Cammous,
    Committee in behalf of Church & Schools
I respectfully present this petition to you
asking you to aid my congregation in their
wants as stated

        Thomas T Johnson

Transcription of Document 9

Letter from an African American Church to the Freedmen's Bureau, April 14, 1867

Westmoreland County, Va., near the Hague
April 14th, 1867

Lieut. Henry K.W. Ayres,
    Asst Sup't. B. R. F. & A. L.
       Warsaw, Richmond Co., Va.

Lieut.

We the colored people in the Dist near the Hague have according to you advice given us last Fall went on and have succeeded in erecting one church and school House, and have another in course of erection; and which will be completed early in the coming summer.

All we want now is a teacher and Sabbath School Books and if we could be furnished with common school books it would be of the greatest benefit to us in this our early and first attempt to educate ourselves. We have had to contend against great prejudices held in the Whites but have now succeeded so far well. Our Sabbath School now agoing is very large. Our building which is 22 x 20 is far insufficient to accommodate those who seek for light.

We have appointed Thomas T. Johnson, our present colored minister, to advise with you and he will call upon you for help asked in this letter.

Henry X Lawson
Charles X Jones
Vincent X Kelly
Archable X Kelly
Edmund X Lee
Peter X Hungerford
Luke X Dammous

Committee on behalf of Church & Schools I respectfully present this petition to you asking you to aid my congregation in their wants as stated.

Thomas T. Johnson

Historical Background

The petition to the Freedmen's Bureau on behalf of an African American congregation in Reconstruction Virginia (document 9) illustrates the central role of black churches in the lives of the newly emancipated African Americans. By the mid-19th century, the black church had long been a unifying force among black Americans, serving, C. Eric Lincoln (1984) has written, as "the black man's government, his social club, his secret order, his espionage system, his political party, and his impetus to freedom and revolution."

The Black Church During Reconstruction

With freedom came the desire of African Americans to establish church organizations independent of white churches and to build houses of worship that would also be schools, social centers, and meeting places for the community. Hundreds of new black churches were established throughout the country.

As one of the few areas of black life little controlled or influenced by the whites during the slavery era, the black church provided talented blacks with opportunities for leadership. Black ministers like Thomas Johnson emerged as the first recognized leaders of the freedmen. During Reconstruction, the African American churches were a major source of support for the freedmen, providing education and relief throughout the South.

The Freedmen's Bureau and the Churches

The petition reproduced here is a letter from Thomas T. Johnson on behalf of his congregation, requesting aid for their church and school from the Bureau of Refugees, Freedmen, and Abandoned Lands. The Freedmen's Bureau was created by Congress in 1865 in part to assist the emancipated African Americans in the transition from slavery to freedom. Though greatly understaffed and underfinanced, the bureau managed in the seven years of its existence to provide some $6 million for schools and education and about $15 million for food and other aid for freed slaves and white and black refugees throughout the South.

Major General Oliver Howard, commissioner of the Freedmen's Bureau, made education a priority. Working with northern relief agencies, most of them church supported, the bureau opened schools in all of the southern states. Already in 1865 some 200 teachers were instructing nearly 13,000 black students.

Bureau support for these schools came from monies appropriated by Congress for "rent and repair" of school buildings and from funds realized from confiscated Confederate property. Teachers' salaries were mostly paid by the private freedmen's aid societies and, in some places, a small tuition. This joint operation of the schools necessitated close cooperation between the bureau and the missionary societies of the northern churches.

The Desire for Education in Virginia

African Americans in Virginia, the home of Thomas Johnson's congregation, were particularly anxious for education. In the year of Johnson's letter, 1867, Virginia freedmen contributed to the support of 155 schools and completely sustained 58. By 1870 they contributed to the support of 215 schools and owned 111 buildings. The enthusiasm for education among the freedmen may be measured by the great sacrifices made by an impoverished people to maintain schools and pay teachers.

As the petition indicates, the Freedmen's Bureau in Virginia encouraged the establishment of schools. Despite the fact that the bureau had very limited resources, some money was provided for buildings, books, and other needs. According to bureau records, 20,000 blacks learned to read in Virginia between 1865 and 1870. (The bureau estimated that in 1866 there were some 500,000 African Americans in the total population of 1,200,000 Virginians.)

In their letter, Johnson's congregation informed the bureau that a new building was under construction. They needed books for both their "common" and sabbath schools and a teacher. The bureau had funds to assist with construction and to provide books, but relied on private relief agencies to supply teachers. By 1867, the shortage of qualified teachers was so acute that Commissioner Howard worked out a plan to aid the benevolent societies, principally the nondenominational American Missionary Association, in establishing teacher-training institutions. This initiative contributed significantly to the founding of many colleges and universities, including Howard, Fisk, and Atlanta universities.

Opposition to Education for the Freedmen

There was, as Johnson's congregation notes, considerable white opposition to the work of the Freedmen's Bureau during the painful period of Reconstruction. Many Virginians strongly resisted the efforts of the bureau to protect and educate former slaves, especially after Congress extended the power of the bureau in 1866. The Ku Klux Klan gained strength; a number of black schools and churches were attacked and destroyed.

Much of the opposition to the education of African Americans centered on the teachers. Even among southern whites favorably disposed to black education, there was considerable resentment toward the teachers in the bureau's schools. Many whites feared that northern teachers would propagate ideas inimical to southern interests. Since most leaders of the freedmen's aid societies were leading abolitionists, it was feared that the teachers they hired would spread ideas of social equality, civil rights, and black suffrage. Such fears were exacerbated by the political activity of some bureau agents and teachers on behalf of the Republican party.

Ironically, opposition to the teachers in bureau schools led some southerners to find southern teachers to replace those from the North. If blacks are to be educated and if they are to vote, some argued, they should be taught by people sympathetic to southern interests.

With the end of Reconstruction, control of black education shifted from the Freedmen's Bureau and the churches to the states. In 1870, Virginia reentered the Union, ending the authority of the bureau there. The new state constitution required the establishment of public free schools. Separate schools were created for blacks, and these soon replaced the bureau schools. Intimidation and repression greatly curtailed the educational and political gains begun in Reconstruction.

African American churches, however, have continued to play a central role in the lives of black people in the South and elsewhere. And African American leadership still emerges from the churches, as evidenced in recent decades by Martin Luther King, Jr., and other leaders in the struggle for civil rights. To again quote C. Eric Lincoln, "the Black Church, like the living faith it represents, has managed for over two hundred years to survive obstruction within and without, and it sill endures as the symbol of the hope and determination of the new black estate in America."

References

Lincoln, C. Eric. (1984). *Race, Religion and the Continuing American Dilemma.* New York: Hill and Wang.

Suggestions for Using the Document

Discussion Questions

1. What can be learned about the people writing this letter from the language used and the manner in which the letter is signed?
2. What does the letter tell us about the freedmen's interest in education?
3. Why did the leadership of the African American community come primarily from ministers?
4. How might the requests in the letter conflict with current interpretations of the No Establishment Clause of the First Amendment by the Supreme Court?
5. Why was the church the most significant institution in African American life?
6. Why do you think newly freed slaves were overwhelmingly enthusiastic about education?
7. Most of the teachers who taught freedmen in the South were women. Why do you think these women endured low salaries and poor living conditions to bring education to the newly freed slaves? How is this significant for understanding the role of women in American history?
8. Discuss the tensions between southern blacks and whites during Reconstruction. Why were many whites opposed to education for blacks?

Extension Activities

1. Arrange for a field trip to a church that serves a predominately African American congregation. Discuss with the minister and members of the congregation the role of the church in the community. If a field trip cannot be arranged, invite the minister and other congregation leaders to visit the class.
2. Show videotapes of speeches by key African American leaders of the Civil Rights Movement. Have the class, working in small groups, identify and discuss the religious references and influences they discover in the speeches.

Research Topics

1. Identify the leadership of the African American community today.
    How many have roots in the black church? What role does reli-
    gious belief play in the lives of the African American leaders?
2. Investigate the work of the Freedmen's Bureau during Reconstruc-
    tion. What was the relationship between the churches, North and
    South, and the bureau?
3. Examine the work of the American Missionary Association. Discuss
    why so many northern churches supported the work of the AMA.
    What were the religious motivations for this work?
4. What was the Black Convention Movement and how did the
    African American churches support that movement?
5. How did the white churches in the South respond to the chal-
    lenges of Reconstruction?

Additional Resources

Anti-Defamation League. The League distributes materials about the
    KKK for classroom use, including *The Ku Klux Klan: An American
    Paradox*, a 20-minute filmstrip that covers the history of the Klan,
    and *Ku Klux Klan: The Invisible Empire*, a powerful CBS documen-
    tary film.

Foner, Eric. (1988). *Reconstruction: America's Unfinished Revolution,
    1863–1877*. New York: Harper & Row. An excellent study of the
    Reconstruction Period.

Nelson, Hart M., Raytha Yokley, and Anne Nelson, eds. (1971). *The
    Black Church in America*. New York: Basic. A collection of essays
    with valuable insights concerning the role of the black church in
    American history.

Social Studies School Service, Culver City, California, distributes a
    number of filmstrips on African American history.

7

No Religious Test

A letter from William Howard Taft on his religious beliefs, 1899, and a press release from Theodore Roosevelt on religious discrimination, 1908

ocument 10

tter to his brother from William Howard Taft on his religious beliefs, 1899

rce: Papers of William Howard Taft, Library of Congress,
hington, D.C.

[Handwritten letter:]

Jany [...]

My dear Harry, (W. TAFT)

Your letter of the 14th instant was duly received, ~~but~~ I have delayed ~~answering~~ a reply not because ~~I am~~ hesitate as to my answers to your questions, but because I wish ~~~~ to express my reasons for ~~th~~ them with some care.

There are two insuperable objections to my accepting an election to the Presidency of Yale University. The first is ~~the religious objection~~ ~~objection found~~ is my religious views. The second is that I am not qualified to discharge ~~ I meet what in spite of ~~ the most im- portant duties of the office.

First— Yale finds ~~its strongest~~ her strongest support in this country among those who believe in the creed of the Orthodox evangelical ~~the~~ churches. ~~the~~ No step should be taken

Document 10 (continued)

which would deprive her of that ~~supper~~ aid.
It is, of course, not necessary that the next
President should be an ordained Minister
of ~~any~~ religion. Indeed I think it would
be a wise departure from a harrowing
tradition if a layman should be chosen.
But it would shock the large conservative
element of those who give Yale her power
and influence in the country to see one
chosen to the Presidency who could not subscribe to the creed of the Orthodox Congregational
Church of New England. ~~If suppising~~ the
election of such a one were possible, it would
provoke a bitterness of feeling and a suspicion
of his every act among those with whom he
would have to cooperate in the discharge
his duties that would deprive him of all
usefulness ~~to the college~~ and would be seriously
detrimental to the University. I believe in God.

cument 10 (continued)

I am a Unitarian. I do not believe in the divinity of Christ, and there are many other of the postulates of the Or. thodox creed to which I can not subscribe. I am not, however, a scoffer at religion but on the contrary, recognize, in the fullest manner the elevating influence that it has had, and always will have, in the history of mankind. I know that it is essential to satisfy the spiritual cravings of human nature and that, merely from an earthly standpoint, it is of supreme importance ~~~~~~~~ in the betterment of the body politic to encourage, religious thought and a religious worship on the part of all the people. I have said this much to show that ~~~~~~ were I President of Yale University, it would be farthest from my impulses to do anything to interfere with the religious life and thought of the students, and the University at large. But ~~~~~~ this

Document 10 (continued)

attitude of my mind toward the religion of
Yale would not be enough to satisfy the views
of those who make up the majority of
her friends, her supporters and her faculties.
In every progressive step taken or suggested by me as
President, I should ~~surmount the must not~~
~~the hearty cooperation of those~~ have first
overcome the unconscious distrust of those
~~faith~~ whose cooperation would be indispensable,
— a ~~before a~~ distrust due wholly to the fact ~~knowledge~~
that I was not ~~an orthodox Christian~~ believer
in the orthodox Christian faith. Such a ~~position~~
~~would be intolerable and I could not~~
~~undertake to discharge~~ condition would be,
not only very harmful to the best interests
of the University but also intolerable to
me.

anscription of Document 10

ter to his brother from William Howard Taft on his religious beliefs

copy

Jan'y. 23rd. 1899

My Dear Harry:—

Your letter of the 14th. instant was duly received. I have delayed a reply not because I hesitate as to my answers to your questions, but because I wish to express my reasons for them with some care.

There are two insuperable objections to my accepting an election to the Presidency of Yale University. The first is my religious views. The second is that I am not qualified to discharge the most important duties of the office.

First—Yale finds her strongest support in this country among those who believe in the creed of the Orthodox Evangelical Churches. No step should be taken which would deprive her of that aid. It is, of course, not necessary that the next President should be an ordained minister of religion. Indeed I think it would be a wise departure from a narrowing tradition if a layman should be chosen. But it would shock the large conservative element of those who give Yale her power and influence in the country to see one chosen to the Presidency who could not subscribe to the creed of the Orthodox Congregational Church of New England. If the election of such a one were possible, it would provoke a bitterness of feeling and a suspicion of his every act among those with whom he would have to cooperate in the discharge of his duties that would deprive him of all usefulness and would be seriously detrimental to the University.

I am a Unitarian. I believe in God. I do not believe in the divinity of Christ, and there are many other of the postulates of the Orthodox creed to which I can not subscribe. I am not, however, a scoffer at religion but on the contrary, recognize in the fullest manner the elevating influence that it has had and always will have in the history of mankind. I know that it is essential to satisfy the spiritual craving of human nature and that, merely from an earthly standpoint, it is of supreme importance in the betterment of the body politic to encourage religious thought and religious worship on the part of all the people. I have said this much to show that were I President of Yale University, it would be farthest from my impulse to do anything to interfere with the religious life and thought of the students and the University at large. But this attitude of my mind toward the religion of Yale would not be enough to satisfy the views of those who make up the majority of her friends, her supporters and her faculties. In every progressive step taken or suggested by me as President, I should have first to overcome the unconscious distrust of those whose cooperation would be indispensable,—a distrust due wholly to the fact that I was not a believer in the Orthodox Christian faith. Such a condition would be not only very harmful to the best interests of the University but also intolerable to me.

Document 11

A press release from Theodore Roosevelt on religious discrimination, 1908

Source: Papers of Theodore Roosevelt, Library of Congress, Washington, D.C.

November 6, 1908.

My dear Sir:

I have received your letter running in part as follows:

"While it is claimed almost universally that religion should not enter into politics, yet there is no denying that it does, and the mass of the voters that are not Catholics will not support a man for any office, especially for President of the United States, who is a Roman Catholic.

"Since Taft has been nominated for President by the Republican party, it is being circulated and is constantly urged as a reason for not voting for Taft that he is an infidel (Unitarian) and his wife and brother Roman Catholics. * * * If his feelings are in sympathy with the Roman Catholic church on account of his wife and brother being Catholics, that would be objectionable to a sufficient number of voters to defeat him. On the other hand if he is an infidel, that would be sure to mean defeat. * * * I am writing this letter for the sole purpose of giving Mr. Taft an opportunity to let the world know what his religious belief is."

I received many ▓▓▓▓▓▓ such letters as yours during the campaign, expressing dissatisfaction with Mr. Taft on religious grounds; some of them on the ground that he was a Unitarian, and others on the ground that he was suspected to be in sympathy with Catholics. I did not answer any of these letters during the campaign because I regarded it as an outrage even to agitate such a question as a man's religious convictions, with the purpose of influencing a political election. But now that the campaign is over, when there is opportunity for men calmly to consider whither such propositions as those you make in your letter would lead, I wish to invite them to consider them, and I have selected your letter to answer because you advance both the objections

cument 11 (continued)

commonly urged against Mr. Taft, namely: that he is a Unitarian, and also
that he is suspected of sympathy with the Catholics.

You ask that Mr. Taft shall "let the world know what his religious belief
is." This is purely his own private concern; it is a matter between him and
his Maker, a matter for his own conscience; and to require it to be made public under penalty of political discrimination is to negative the first principles
of our Government, which guarantee complete religious liberty, and the right to
each man to act in religious affairs as his own conscience dictates. Mr. Taft
never asked my advice in the matter, but if he had asked it, I should have em-
phatically advised him against thus stating publicly his religious belief. The
demand for a statement of a candidate's religious belief can have no meaning
except that there may be discrimination for or against him because of that belief. Discrimination against the holder of one faith means retaliatory discrimination against men of other faiths. The inevitable result of entering
upon such a practise would be an abandonment of our real freedom of conscience
and a reversion to the dreadful conditions of religious dissension which in so
many lands have proved fatal to true liberty, to true religion, and to all
advance in civilization.

To discriminate against a thoroly uprightcitizen because he belongs to
some particular church, or because, like Abraham Lincoln, he has not avowed
his allegiance to any church, is an outrage against that liberty of conscience
which is one of the foundations of American life. You are entitled to know
whether a man seeking your suffrages is a man of clean and upright life,
honorable in all his dealings with his fellows, and fit by qualification and purpose to do well in the great office for which he is a candidate; but you are not entitled to know matters which lie purely between
himself and his Maker. If it is proper or legitimate to oppose a man

Document 11 (continued)

for being a Unitarian, as was John Quincy Adams, for instance, as is
the Rev. Edward Everett Hale, at the present moment Chaplain of the Senate, and an American whose life all good Americans are proud - then
it would be equally proper to support or oppose a man because of his
views on justification by faith, or the method of administering the
sacrament, or the gospel of salvation by works.   If you once enter on
such a career there is absolutely no limit at which you can legitimate-
ly stop.

So much for your objections to Mr. Taft because he is a Unitarian.
Now, for your objections to him because you think his wife and brother
to be Roman Catholics.   As it happens, they are not; but if they were,
or if he were a Roman Catholic himself, it ought not to affect in the
slightest degree any man's supporting him for the position of President.
You say that "the mass of the voters that are not Catholics will not
support a man for any office, especially for President of the United
States, who is a Roman Catholic."   I believe that when you say this
you foully slander your fellow countrymen.   I do not for one moment
believe that the mass of our fellow citizens, or that any considerable
number of our fellow citizens, can be influenced by such narrow bigotry
as to refuse to vote for any thoroly upright and fit man because he
happens to have a particular religious creed.   Such a consideration
should never be treated as a reason for either supporting or opposing a
candidate for a political office.   Are you aware that there are several
States in this Union where the majority of the people are now Catholics?
I should reprobate in the severest terms the Catholics who in those
States (or in any other States) refused to vote for the most fit man
because he happened to be a Protestant; and my condemnation would be

cument 11 (continued)

4

exactly as severe for Protestants who, under reversed circumstances, refused to vote for a Catholic.   In public life I am happy to say that I have known many men who were elected, and constantly reelected, to office in districts where the great majority of their constituents were of a different religious belief.   I knew Catholics who have for many years represented constituencies mainly Protestant, and Protestants who have for many years represented constituencies mainly Catholic; and among the Congressmen whom I knew particularly well was one man of Jewish faith who represented a district in which there were hardly any Jews at all.   All of these men by their very existence in political life refute the slander you have uttered against your fellow Americans.

I believe that this Republic will endure for many centuries.   If so there will doubtless be among its Presidents Protestants and Catholics, and very probably at some time, Jews.   I have consistently tried while President to act in relation to my fellow Americans of Catholic faith as I hope that any future President who happens to be a Catholic will act towards his fellow Americans of Protestant faith.   Had I followed any other course I should have felt that I was unfit to represent the American people.

In my Cabinet at the present moment there sit side by side Catholic and Protestant, Christian and Jew, each man chosen because in my belief he is peculiarly fit to exercise on behalf of all our people the duties of the office to which I have appointed him.   In no case does the man's religious belief in any way influence his discharge of his duties, save

Document 11 (continued)

5

as it makes him more eager to act justly and uprightly in his relations to all men.   The same principles that have obtained in appointing the members of my Cabinet, the highest officials under me, the officials to whom is entrusted the work of carrying out all the important policies of my administration, are the principles upon which all good Americans should act in choosing, whether by election or appointment, the man to fill any office from the highest totthe lowest in the land.

Yours truly,

(signed) Theodore Roosevelt

Mr. J. C. Martin,
    Corner Courth and Jefferson Streets,
    Dayton, Ohio.

Historical Background

No religious test shall ever be required as a qualification to any office or public trust under the United States.

—U.S. Constitution, Article VI

When the Constitutional Convention of 1787 adopted Article VI as part of the U.S. Constitution, a major victory was won for the cause of religious liberty. The new nation had broken with a centuries-old tradition and prohibited any kind of religious test for national office.

The constitutional prohibition against religious tests did not, however, open the door for people of all faiths or none to hold office in the federal government. For much of our history, many voters have successfully applied an unofficial but powerful test, particularly in presidential elections, that has required candidates to profess the Protestant faith. This barrier was not overcome on the presidential level until the election of John Kennedy in 1960.

Religion in the Campaign of 1908

The campaign of 1908 provides an interesting case study for understanding the role of religious tests in national contests. In that election, President Theodore Roosevelt had orchestrated the nomination of William Howard Taft to run on the Republican ticket against Democrat William Jennings Bryan. One of the underlying issues throughout the campaign was Taft's religious faith.

The first source of antipathy toward Taft by many American Protestants was his actions as civil governor of the Philippines in the 1890s. Taft had negotiated with the Vatican to settle claims for land taken from friars in the Philippines. News of these negotiations was greeted with outrage by some Protestants who saw Taft as giving in to the Pope of the Roman Catholic Church by recommending the payment of large sums of money for church properties. Taft's contact with the Vatican was resurrected and expanded in the 1908 campaign, as rumors circulated that he favored Catholics in the settlement. He was even "charged" (inaccurately) with having Catholic relatives.

Taft was also strongly attacked for being a Unitarian, a faith viewed with antagonism and suspicion by some Protestant voters.[1] President Roosevelt received hundreds of letters demanding to know whether the Republican nominee rejected Christ. "Think of the United States with a President who does not believe that Jesus Christ was the Son of God," wrote the editor of one religious paper, "but looks upon our immaculate Savior as a common bastard and low, cursing impostor."

The Taft campaign quietly assured the public that Taft, although a Unitarian, was a good Christian. Press stories began to appear emphasizing that Mrs. Taft was an Episcopalian and that their daughter had been confirmed in that faith. Taking Roosevelt's private advice, Taft made no public declaration of his beliefs. During the campaign, he wrote to a friend explaining why he was saying little about the matter:

> Of course, I am interested in the spread of Christian civilization, but to go into a dogmatic discussion of creed I will not do whether I am defeated or not. . . . If the American electorate is so narrow as not to elect a Unitarian, well and good. I can stand it (Papers of William Howard Taft).

Taft's Religious Beliefs and the Protestant Revival

Fortunately for Taft's campaign, another letter, written nine years earlier to his brother Henry Taft (document 10), was not made public during the campaign. Under discussion was his nomination for another presidency, that of Yale University. Through his brother, he informed Yale that he could not serve because of his religious views. "I do not believe in the divinity of Christ, and there are many other of the postulates of the Orthodox creed to which I can not subscribe." The "orthodoxy" Taft referred to was the Congregational Church, until 1818 the established church of Connecticut.

Just as it would have shocked "the large conservative element of those who give Yale her power and influence" to see a Unitarian chosen as university president, so it would have shocked many in the nation to have a president who denied the divinity of Christ. Taft was well aware of how much his views offended more traditional Protestants. Perhaps that is why the draft of his letter reveals the addition of several phrases, including "I believe in God," that strengthen the letter's religious content.

---

[1] The Unitarian faith, represented today in the Unitarian Universalist Association, is based on the free search for truth. Members generally affirm God as the source of mind and spirit, but vary widely in their views concerning Jesus. Unitarians place great emphasis on justice, peace, and universal brotherhood and sisterhood.

The early 20th century was not a propitious time for an American politician to be unorthodox in his religious views. Many Evangelical Protestants were fighting back against theological liberalism and Darwinism. For these Christians, it was not sufficient to hold Taft's view that religion has an "elevating influence" that satisfies "the spiritual cravings of human nature." It was time, they believed, to reject the evils of modern thinking and to reaffirm what they viewed as the fundamental truths of Christianity: the Scriptures, Virgin Birth, Resurrection, First Atonement, and the Second Coming of Christ. Such reaffirmations formed the basis for the fundamentalist movement that has become such a significant force in the political and social life of America in the second half of the 20th century.

A Resurgence of Nativism

Attacks on Taft's religious views and Catholic sympathies were politically potent because of the resurgence of nativism in the late 19th and early 20th centuries. Millions of new immigrants poured into the cities, forcing the nation to confront unprecedented social, economic, and political challenges. As the immigrant population grew, swelling the ranks of the Catholic Church, the nativists' fears of the pre–Civil War period returned in full force. The new arrivals were seen as alien threats to American values, competition for American jobs, and most worrisome of all, a potential bloc vote that could determine national elections.[2]

Hate groups like the American Protective Association led the fight against what they believed to be a "papal threat" to destroy democracy. Spurious stories, often featuring the Irish, were spread throughout the country about Catholic plots to overthrow the government and attack Protestants. Irish Catholic political successes in cities like Chicago and Boston only reinforced the fears of the APA and similar groups.

One of the most extreme leaders of the anti-Catholic movement was Senator Thomas Watson of Georgia. He helped spread Maria Monk's discredited writings about the "horrors" of convent life and even published a sequel to the book. Once again, fabricated stories of sexual abuse and murder by priests and nuns fueled the fires of fear and bigotry. Watson carried his hate campaign into presidential politics, running for president on the Populist ticket in 1904 and 1908.

---

[2]For a discussion of the origins of nativism see Chapter 4.

Theodore Roosevelt's Response

The political clout enjoyed by the nativists of the 1850s was duplicated In some local contests in the early 20th century. On a national level, however, the extreme anti-Catholic position failed to poll many votes. Senator Watson received a mere 150,000 votes in his two tries for the presidency. Though nativist fears remained widespread, by 1908 many Protestant Americans had come to accept the Roman Catholic Church as an American church. The Catholic Church had become part of the fabric of American life. Catholics had, for example, become increasingly visible as leaders in the labor movement and other efforts for social justice.

In his press release of November 6, 1908 (document 11), President Roosevelt signaled the nation's growing acceptance of a new pluralism in America. Roosevelt's statement to the press was given in the form of a reply to one of the many letters he had received attacking Taft as an "infidel (Unitarian)" and as a man "in sympathy with the Roman Catholic church." With Taft safely elected, the president took the opportunity to place in the public record his abhorrence of such sentiments.

Roosevelt strongly rejected the idea that a candidate's faith has any relationship to fitness for public office. Voters are entitled to know if the candidate has led a "clean and upright life," but religious belief is between the individual and God, "a matter for his own conscience." Ever the smart politician, Roosevelt was careful to add that Abraham Lincoln avowed alliance to no church and John Quincy Adams was a Unitarian.

President Roosevelt made it clear that he understood religious liberty in America to be among the "first principles" of our government, the guarantee of "our real freedom of conscience." Without these principles to protect the conscience of each citizen, the nation would see a "reversion to the dreadful conditions of religious dissension which in so many lands have proved fatal to true liberty."

In the letter, the president also defined religious liberty as a kind of Golden Rule for civic life. "I have consistently tried while President to act in relation to my fellow Americans of Catholic faith as I hope that any future President who happens to be a Catholic will act towards his fellow Americans of Protestant faith." In other words, our rights are best guaranteed when the rights of all citizens are protected.

Roosevelt's strong defense of freedom of conscience was a powerful and much-needed reminder to the nation that the principles of liberty embodied in Article VI and the First Amendment are the ground rules that enable people of many faiths to live together as one nation. Needless to say, however, the struggle to live out those principles would continue. Religious tests would still be applied by some voters in national politics, most notably in the campaign of 1928. And nativist fears and resentments would help to pass increasingly restrictive and discriminatory immigration laws over the vetoes of both President Taft and President Wilson.

References
Papers of William Howard Taft. Washington, D.C.: Library of Congress.

Suggestions for Using the Documents

Discussion Questions

1. Discuss the changes Taft made in his draft letter. Why do you think he inserted these additional comments about his religious belief?
2. What do you think would have happened if Taft's letter had been made public during the 1908 campaign? What would happen today if a similar letter came to light involving a presidential candidate?
3. Can someone who does not accept the divinity of Christ win the presidency today? What about an avowed atheist? Roosevelt mentioned in his press release that the country may one day have a Jewish president. Is that possible today?
4. Should the religious beliefs of a candidate ever be an issue in an election campaign?
5. What has been the role of religious belief in recent presidential campaigns?
6. Roosevelt states that voters are entitled to know if a candidate is a person of "clean and upright life." How much about a candidate's personal life do you think the electorate is entitled to know?
7. In his letter to President Roosevelt, J. C. Martin states that non-Catholics will not vote for a Roman Catholic. Roosevelt refutes that claim. Was Roosevelt right? Could a Roman Catholic have been elected president in 1908?
8. Roosevelt issued this press release after the election. He also would have advised Taft not to discuss his religious beliefs during the campaign. Do you agree that this was the best way to handle the rumors? Would it have been better for Roosevelt to have issued the press release before the election?

Extension Activities

1. Ask the class to look in recent newspapers and magazines for examples of religion in the political life of the United States and other nations. Have students compare the relationship between religion and politics in different parts of the world.
2. Divide the class into groups, each of which is to act as advisors to an imaginary political candidate with specific religious or nonreligious convictions (for example, Jewish, atheist, religion unknown). Present these scenarios:

    *   Your candidate will be asked in a debate if he or she is "born again." How do you advise your candidate to answer that question?
    *   In the midst of the campaign, rumors circulate about your candidate's religious views. Draft a press release that you think will be most helpful to the election of your candidate.

Research Topics

1. Explore recent efforts by Christian Voice and other groups to encourage people to vote for "Christian" candidates. Write a position paper on why you support or oppose such efforts. How successful have these efforts been?
2. Examine the campaigns of Al Smith and John Kennedy. How did these candidates handle the issue of their religion?
3. What are the origins of the Unitarian Church in the United States?

Additional Resources

Handy, Robert T. (1971). *A Christian America: Protestant Hopes and Historical Realities*. New York: Oxford University Press. An excellent study of the "Protestant era" of American history.

Higham, John. (1975). *Strangers in the Land: Patterns of American Nativism, 1860–1925*. New York: Atheneum. One of the best discussions of nativism and politics in the United States.

8

The School Prayer Controversy

A memorandum from William O. Douglas
to Hugo Black on *Engel v. Vitale*, 1962

Document 12

Memorandum from William O. Douglas to Hugo Black, June 11, 1962

Source: Papers of William O. Douglas, Library of Congress, Washington, D.C. Used by permission of the estate of William O. Douglas.

cc Conf.

Dear Hugo

As you know I have

had troubles with No 468 Engel
vs Vitale

I have put my

troubles on paper — not
with the view of filing a
concurrence or a dissent but
in order to [illegible] define the

Document 12 (continued)

serious issue that seems
to me involved

I am sending a copy
of this memo to the other
Brethren

I am inclined
to reverse if we
are prepared to
disallow public property and
public funds to be used
to finance a religious welfare

ocument 12 (continued)

If however we would strike down a New York requirement that public school teachers open ~~with~~ each day with prayer I think we could not consistently open each of our sessions with ~~the~~ prayer. That's the Kernel of my problem

W W

Transcription of Document 12

A memorandum from William O. Douglas to Hugo Black, June 11, 1962

cc Conf.

Dear Hugo

As you know, I have had troubles with No. 468—*Engel* v. *Vitale*.

I have put my troubles on paper—not with the view of filing a concurrence or a dissent but in order to define the narrow issue that seems to me involved.

I am sending a copy of this memo to the other Brethren.

I am inclined to reverse if we are prepared to disallow public property and public funds to be used to finance a religious exercise.

If, however, we would strike down a New York requirement that public school teachers open each day with prayer, I think we could not consistently open each of our sessions with prayer. That's the kernel of my problem.

(William O. Douglas)

Historical Background

In the 1950s, the State Board of Regents in New York authorized local school districts to order the recitation of the following prayer at the beginning of each school day:

> Almighty God, we acknowledge our dependence upon Thee, and we beg thy blessings upon us, our parents, our teachers, and our Country.

The Regents' prayer was adopted in 1958 by the Board of Education of Union Free School District No. 9 in New Hyde Park, New York. Schools were directed to have the prayer said aloud by each class in the presence of a teacher at the beginning of each school day. Children unwilling to recite the prayer were to be excused from participation or permitted to absent themselves from the classroom on written request from their parents.

In 1959 parents of ten children in the New Hyde Park schools sought a court order to compel the school district to discontinue recitation of the prayer. The parents argued that state-sponsored prayer in schools was contrary to their religious beliefs and a violation of the No Establishment Clause of the First Amendment. The lower state courts and the New York Court of Appeals upheld the power of New York to mandate prayer in schools as long as the schools did not compel any student to join in the prayer.

The case, known as *Engel v. Vitale*, was appealed to the Supreme Court of the United States. On June 25, 1962, the Supreme Court, in a six to one decision (two justices did not participate), reversed the judgment of the Court of Appeals, ruling that "by using its public school system to encourage recitation of the Regents' prayer, the State of New York has adopted a practice wholly inconsistent with the Establishment Clause."

Religion in the Schools

The role of religion in the New York public schools has been a subject of much controversy from the beginning of the common school movement. Nineteenth century Protestants strongly supported the new system of universal free public education, taking for granted that the schools would transmit Christian (Protestant) morality and ideals. The first public schools were infused with Protestant practices and beliefs.

Not surprisingly, people of other faiths complained about the Protestant hegemony in the schools. In 1843, for example, a group of Jewish parents in New York objected to the Christian teachings that filled the textbooks. A committee was appointed to examine the matter, but it did not seem to grasp the nature of the objection. The committee rejected the protest, reporting to the board of Education that it had

> examined the several passages and lessons alluded to and had been unable to discern any ground of objection, even by the Jews, except what may arise from the fact that they are chiefly derived from the New Testament and inculcate the general principles of Christ (Grinstein 1945).

The strongest complaints in New York came from the growing Roman Catholic community. Protestant religious instruction (including readings from the King James version of the Scriptures) and anti-Catholic references in the textbooks alienated Catholics from the public schools and contributed to the founding and growth of the parochial school movement.

Sectarian instruction was eventually prohibited in New York public schools. Bible reading and prayer, however, were allowed to remain, vestiges of Protestantism as a dominant cultural force. The Supreme Court rulings of 1962 and 1963 came as a shock to many Americans who had long assumed that Christian, particularly Protestant Christian, values and symbols represented the heart of the American way of life and American institutions.

The Majority Opinion

The New York Regents had taken care to compose a prayer that they believed would be "subscribed to by all men and women of good will." By the 1960s, however, the Protestant-Catholic-Jewish mainstream that might have once agreed to such a prayer was no longer a sufficient definition for American pluralism. Consensus on public expressions of piety had become much more difficult in a nation that now included many new religions and growing numbers of nonbelievers.

The emergence of a new pluralism in America and the erosion of the traditional Protestant cultural hegemony was reflected in the Supreme Court's interpretations of the No Establishment Clause in the early 1960s. For some Americans, the movement toward a religiously plural society and a more secular government was the fulfillment of the First Amendment's promise to disestablish religion. For others, the Court was shifting from an America "under God" to an America without God.

Writing for the majority in *Engel v. Vitale* (1962), Associate Justice Hugo Black interpreted the First Amendment as building Jefferson's "wall" between church and state:

> The petitioners contend among other things that the state laws requiring or permitting use of the Regents' prayer must be struck

down as a violation of the Establishment Clause because that prayer was composed by governmental officials as a part of a governmental program to further religious beliefs. For this reason, petitioners argue, the State's use of the Regents' prayer in its public school system breaches the constitutional wall of separation between Church and State. We agree with that contention since we think that the constitutional prohibition against laws respecting an establishment of religion must at least mean that in this country it is no part of the business of government to compose official prayers for any group of the American people to recite as a part of a religious program carried on by government.

The majority supported its opinion by an appeal to history. Freedom from governmentally composed prayers, argued Black, was one of the reasons many early American colonists left England in the first place. The First Amendment was added to the Constitution to ensure that no American government could determine the religious practices of the American people:

> Under that Amendment's prohibition against governmental establishment of religion, as reinforced by the provisions of the Fourteenth Amendment, government in this country, be it state or federal, is without power to prescribe by law any particular form of prayer in carrying on any program of governmentally sponsored religious activity.

That the prayer was "nondenominational" and that those who did not wish to participate were excused did not sway the Court. The program's "constitutional defects" ran deeper:

> The Establishment Clause, unlike the Free Exercise Clause, does not depend upon any showing of direct governmental compulsion and is violated by the enactment of laws which establish an official religion whether those laws operate directly to coerce nonobserving individuals or not. This is not to say, of course, that laws officially prescribing a particular form of religious worship do not involve coercion of such individuals. When the power, prestige and financial support of government is placed behind a particular religious belief, the indirect coercive pressure upon religious minorities to conform to the prevailing officially approved religion is plain. But the purposes underlying the Establishment Clause go much further than that. Its first and most immediate purpose rested on the belief that a union of government and religion tends to destroy government and degrade religion.

Black concluded the majority opinion with the double warning that government involvement with religion weakens religion, and that government endorsement of a particular form of religion leads to religious conflict and persecution. The Court's ruling, he insisted, must not be read as hostility to religion. On the contrary, just as men of faith had written the First Amendment to put an end to governmental control of prayer, so the Supreme Court was acting to protect faith from governmental intrusion:

> It is neither sacrilegious nor anti-religious to say that each separate government in this country should stay out of the business of writing or sanctioning official prayers and leave that purely religious function to the people themselves and to those the people choose to look to for religious guidance.

Justice Douglas' Concurring Opinion

William Douglas joined with the majority to rule state-sponsored prayer in public schools unconstitutional. But he wrote a concurring opinion in order to define the issue in terms designed to build an even higher "wall of separation."

Douglas indicated his problem with the case in an internal memorandum written to Hugo Black and circulated to the other justices. (A handwritten draft of the memo is reproduced here as document 12.) The "narrow issue" for Douglas was the use of public funds and public property to finance a religious exercise. Douglas was prepared to disallow school prayer on the ground that such financing was unconstitutional, but he wanted the Court to be consistent. In the memo to Black, he put the issue sharply by reminding the brethren that the Supreme Court opens every session with a supplication to God:

> If, however, we would strike down a New York requirement that public school teachers open each day with prayer, I think we could not consistently open each of our sessions with prayer. That's the kernel of my problem.

This private memo of June 11 did not persuade the other justices to adopt a more "consistent" position. The memo is, however, a fascinating glimpse into William Douglas' decision making as he moved to a strongly separationist position. When he delivered his concurring opinion a few days later, he focused on his objection to the use of tax money for *any* religious activity:

> The point for decision is whether the Government can constitutionally finance a religious exercise. Our system at the federal and state levels is presently honeycombed with such financing. Nevertheless, I think it is an unconstitutional undertaking whatever form it takes.

The issue, Douglas insisted, was not compulsion to pray or proselytizing in the schools. He found evidence of neither in the *Engel* case. The issue was the use of public money to finance religion. Douglas had reached the conclusion that all such financing, including the salaries of chaplains for state legislatures and Congress, establishes religion in violation of the First Amendment. All such practices, he argued, violate the principle of religious liberty.

This view of the First Amendment represented a shift in Douglas' thinking. In 1952, in delivering the opinion of the Court in *Zorach v. Clauson*, Douglas had supported "released time" in public schools, arguing that a complete separation of church and state was not possible. "A fastidious atheist or agnostic," he wrote, "could even object to the supplication with which the Court opens each session: 'God save the United States and this Honorable Court.'" A decade later, Douglas had become more fastidious himself, asking in *Engel* for a neutrality that keeps the government entirely out of religious matters, including prayers before Court sessions. He summarized his new understanding of the First Amendment this way:

> The First Amendment leaves the Government in a position not of hostility to religion but of neutrality. The philosophy is that the atheist or agnostic—the nonbeliever—is entitled to go his own way. The philosophy is that if the government interferes in matters spiritual, it will be a divisive force. The First Amendment teaches that a government neutral in the field of religion better serves all religious interests.

Potter Stewart Dissents

The lone dissent in *Engel v. Vitale* came from Justice Stewart. He saw the issue as simply "letting those who want to say a prayer say it." To deny children the opportunity to recite the Regents' prayer "is to deny them the opportunity of sharing in the spiritual heritage of our Nation."

Stewart rejected the contention of the majority that the New York authorities had established "an official religion." The very practices that Douglas described in his concurring opinion as violative of the No Establishment Clause Stewart viewed as evidence that religious traditions are a part of the fabric of our nation and thus have a place in our governmental institutions:

> At the opening of each day's Session of this Court we stand, while one of our officials invokes the protection of God. Since the days of John Marshall our Crier has said, "God save the United States and this Honorable Court." Both the Senate and the House of Representatives open their daily Sessions with prayer.

What Douglas saw as inconsistencies, Stewart viewed as "highly cherished spiritual traditions." The government, Stewart pointed out, has prescribed religious language many times, adding "under God" to the Pledge of Allegiance in 1954 and "In God We Trust" to our coins in 1865 and calling upon the president to proclaim a National Day of Prayer in 1952. Stewart summarized his argument using Douglas' own words from *Zorach*: "We are a religious people whose institutions presuppose a Supreme Being." In both of their opinions, Stewart and

Douglas called upon the majority to be consistent. For Douglas, consistency would require that not one cent of tax money be used to support religion. Stewart, however, believed that consistency would mean allowing public schools to do what Congress and the Court do at the beginning of each session.

The Debate Continues

The decision in *Engel v. Vitale* was followed a year later by a similar decision in *School District of Abington Township v. Schempp* prohibiting Bible reading as a devotional exercise in public schools. These cases proved to be only the beginning of the controversy over state-sponsored religious exercises in public schools.

After these two highly unpopular decisions, governors of 49 states called for a constitutional amendment to overturn the Court's rulings. Although no amendment was adopted at that time, efforts continue to get a school prayer amendment through Congress.

References
Grinstein, Hyman B. (1945). *The Rise of the Jewish Community of New York: 1654–1860*. Philadelphia: Jewish Publication Society of America, pp. 235-236.

Suggestions for Using the Document

Discussion Questions

1. A 1985 study indicated that school-sponsored prayer is still recited in 14 percent of the nation's school districts. Discuss why so many schools are defying the Supreme Court decision more than 25 years after *Engel v. Vitale*.
2. After the *Engel v. Vitale* decision was announced by the Supreme Court, many Americans thought that the Court had "banned God from the schools." Did the Court ban all prayer in schools? Are some forms of prayer still permissible? May a student say a prayer before lunch (or before a math test)? Discuss the differences between state-sponsored religious exercises and other forms of prayer in school.
3. Do the Supreme Court decisions concerning school prayer prohibit discussion of religion in public schools? How may religion be discussed in ways that are constitutional?

4. Is there a difference between teacher-led prayer in public schools and prayers given by a chaplain in Congress or in a state legislature? Does the fact that children are involved in the school setting make a difference?

Extension Activities

1. In *Marsh v. Chambers* (1983), the Supreme Court upheld the practice of states hiring a chaplain to offer prayers before legislative sessions. Have students examine the Court's thinking in that decision and answer these questions: Do you agree or disagree? How would you have decided the case?
2. Have students list references to God and religion in practices by government institutions and officials. Ask them which references they think are constitutional or unconstitutional.
3. In 1984 the following school prayer amendment was introduced in Congress: "Nothing in this Constitution shall be construed to prohibit individual or group prayer in public schools or other public institutions. No person shall be required by the United States or by any State to participate in prayer." Have students work in groups to answer the following questions: What would the effect of this amendment be if passed? Would teachers be able to lead classes in a prayer like the New York Regents' prayer? What do you think would happen in your school? Do you support or oppose this amendment?
4. Present students with the following scenario and questions: Your class has been asked to compose a prayer that can be said each morning. What is your immediate reaction? What would you do? Is there a prayer that most students would agree to recite?

Research Topics

1. A number of states have passed laws allowing for a "moment of silence" in public school classrooms each morning. Does your state have such a law? In 1985 the Supreme Court struck down Alabama's moment-of-silence law (*Wallace v. Jaffree*). Examine why that law was ruled unconstitutional. The majority of the justices suggested that future laws mandating a moment of silence might be viewed differently. Why? Do you think a "moment of silence" should be ruled constitutional?
2. Examine the Supreme Court rulings that made the Religious Liberty clauses of the First Amendment applicable to the states through the Fourteenth Amendment.

Additional Resources

Two audiovisual programs for classroom use are:

Religion and Public Schools. (1982). Educational Enrichment Materials. An 11-minute filmstrip focused on prayer in the schools and the teaching of creationism. This fair, if brief, presentation of the issues serves to get a good discussion started. Developed by the National Street Law Institute and distributed by Random House.

The Schempp Case: Bible Reading in Public School. (1969). Chicago: Encyclopaedia Britannica. A 35-minute, 16mm film dramatizing the *School District of Abington Township v. Schempp* case of 1963. This is a useful introduction to the debate over religious exercises in public schools.

The following publications address a broad range of issues concerning religion and public education:

Religion and Public Education is published three times year by the National Council on Religion and Public Education (N162 Lagomarcino Hall, Iowa State University, Ames, Iowa 50011). This outstanding journal is a clearinghouse for the latest news and information about religion studies in public education, including new resources for teaching about religion and current debates about the proper role of religion in the schools.

Sendor, Benjamin. (1988). *A Legal Guide to Religion and Public Education.* Topeka: National Organization on Legal Problems of Education. A comprehensive discussion of what the courts have said about religion and the public schools. Available from the NOLPE at Southwest Plaza, Suite 223, 3061 SW 29th, Topeka, Kansas 66614.

Wood, James F., Jr.,ed. (1985). *Religion, the State, and Education.* Waco, Tex.: Baylor University Press. Nine articles on the role of religion in the public schools.

9

The Needs and Requirements of Muslim Students in Public Schools

A letter from the Islamic Society of North America that is currently sent to many public school officials in the United States

ocument 13

tter from the Islamic Society of North America that is currently sent to many public school officials in the
ed States

rce: Islamic Society of North America, Plainfield, Indiana. Used by permission.

بسم الله الرحمن الرحيم

الإتحاد الإسلامي لدى امريكا الشمالية

THE ISLAMIC SOCIETY OF NORTH AMERICA

NEEDS & REQUIREMENTS OF

MUSLIM STUDENTS

IN PUBLIC SCHOOLS

Dear Sir/Madam:

I would like to bring to your attention some of the most serious
problems faced by Muslim students in public schools. We seek
your urgent cooperation in solving these problems in order to
guarantee religious freedom and non-discrimination.

A.   Please be advised that according to the teachings of Islam as
     enunciated in the Quran, the revealed Book of Allah (God),
     and the traditions of Prophet Muhammad (Peace be upon him),
     all Muslim men and women must abide by the following dress
     code in public:

     (1) Men must cover all parts of their body at least from
         naval to the knee.

     (2) Women must cover all parts of their body except their
         face and hands.

     (3) Both sexes are asked not to wear tight clothing.

     (4) Both sexes must cover private parts of their body even in
         front of their own sex.

Document 13 (continued)

Islam also does not permit unnecessary mixing together for the two sexes.

On behalf of ISNA, the largest organization of Muslims in the United States and Canada, I would like to request that in view of the above teachings of Islam, Muslim students in your school system should not be required to:

Page 2

(1) sit next to the opposite sex in the classroom.

(2) participate in physical education, swimming or dancing classes. Alternate meaningful educational activities should be arranged for them. We urge you to organize physical education and swimming classes separately for boys and girls in accordance with the following guidelines:

a) Separate classes should be held for boys and girls in a fully covered area (no glass doors or windows without curtains).

b) Only male/female instructors for the respective group.

c) Special swimming suits which will cover all the private parts of the body down to the knee.

d) Separate and covered shower facilities for each student.

(3) participate in plays, proms, social parties, picnics, dating, etc. which require free mixing of the two sexes.

(4) participate in any event or activity related to Christmas, Easter, Halloween, or Valentine. All such occasions have religious and social connotations contrary to Islamic faith and teachings.

B. We also urge you to ensure that the following facilities are available to Muslim students in your school:

ocument 13 (continued)

(1) They are excused from their classes to attend off-campus special prayers on Fridays (approximately 1 to 2:00 p.m.).

(2) They are excused for 15 minutes in the afternoon to offer a special prayer in a designated area on the Campus. This prayer is mandatory for all Muslims and often cannot be offered after the school hours.

Page 3

(3) All food items containing meat of a pig (pork, ham, bacon, etc.) in any form and shape (including animal shortening, monogliceride or any other related ingredient) as well as alcohol should be clearly labeled in the cafeteria. Food prepared by vegetable shortening with non-alcohol and pork-free ingredients should be available for a Muslim student.

(4) At least one properly covered toilet should be available in each men's and women's room. The availability of a water pipe in that toilet will also be highly desireable.

(5) Muslim students are excused (without penalty of absence for the two most important festivals of Islam:

Eid Al-Fitr and Eid Al-Adha in accordance with the lunar calendar.

I hope your school system will do its utmost to honor and respect the religious requirements of your Muslim students in order to facilitate their educational process. I will be happy to answer any inquiries from you regarding this matter.

Sincerely,

Sha'ban M. Ismail, Ph.D.
Head of Department of Education

SI/has/Sclprob.doc

Historical Background

The letter reproduced here from the Islamic Society of North America to public school administrators in the United States (document 13) is a dramatic reminder of the strong Muslim presence in America. There are now between three and five million American Muslims.[1] Sometime in the next 30 years Islam will be the second largest religion in the nation, after Christianity.

Worldwide, there are nearly one billion Muslims. Islam is the dominate faith in some 40 countries in a geographic area that extends from sub-Saharan Africa through Indonesia. Clearly, it is essential that Americans be educated about Islam in order to understand important developments in our country and throughout the world.

Islam in America

Although Islam is not usually thought of as an American religion, there are records of Muslims in America as early as the 18th century. In the late 19th and early 20th centuries, significant numbers of Muslims began to migrate to the United States from the Middle East, despite restrictive and discriminatory immigration laws. Recent waves of immigrants have included many Muslims from the Middle East and East Europe, some fleeing political oppression and others seeking economic opportunity. Today, by some estimates, Muslims constitute 14 percent of all immigrants entering the United States.

According to the Middle East Institute in Washington, D.C., as many as one-third of the Muslims in the United States are African Americans whose forebears converted to Islam in the 20th century. This growing Islamic community is adapting and flourishing in the American environment. Its vitality can be seen in the more than 600 Islamic centers across the country.

Nevertheless, American Muslims face a variety of challenges as they practice their faith in this secular and pluralistic society. Islamic law, based on the teachings of the Qur'an,[2] differs from American civil law on such matters as marriage, inheritance, and divorce. Muslims who wish to fulfill the obligations of prayer and observance of religious

---

[1]Estimates of the number of Muslims in the United States vary from 600,000 to 9,000,000. A *Time* article (May 23, 1988) used the figure 4,664,000. The Middle East Institute in Washington, D.C., used the figure 3,000,000 in a 1986 publication.

[2]The Qur'an is the sacred scripture of Islam. Muslims believe that the Qur'an was revealed by Allah through the angel Gabriel (Jibril) to the Prophet Muhammed.

holidays frequently encounter job-related problems. The most disturbing challenge may be the rise in anti-Muslim prejudice fueled by what many Muslims see as unbalanced and insensitive portrayals of Islam in the media.

American Muslims are meeting these challenges by becoming more organized and visible. The largest organization of Muslims in the United States is the Islamic Society of North America, a federation of Islamic organizations and institutions as well as a general membership organization open to any Muslim. The ISNA describes its objectives this way:

> Broadly speaking, the main objective of ISNA is to advance the cause of Islam and Muslims in North America. In pursuance of this, it seeks to foster unity and brotherhood among Muslims and to raise their Islamic consciousness as a people enjoining the right and forbidding wrong; to convey the Islamic message to non-Muslims and to promote friendly relations between them and Muslims.

Requests from the Islamic Society of North America

Document 13, an ISNA letter concerning the "needs and requirements of Muslim students in public schools," is a case study in the practical problems faced by Muslims in American society. It also raises many vital church-state issues public schools are now struggling to resolve.

The letter is sent by Sha'ban M. Ismail, Head of the Department of Education for the ISNA. Ismail opens with an appeal to religious freedom. In the American context, of course, this is a reference to the Free Exercise Clause of the First Amendment.

Ismail then informs administrators about the teachings of Islam concerning the dress code of Muslim men and women in public. Also noted is the fact that Islam "does not permit unnecessary mixing together" of the two sexes. The ISNA wishes schools to know that these teachings are given in the Qur'an and the traditions of the Prophet Muhammad.[3]

The letter then lists the accommodations the ISNA urges that public schools make for Muslim students. The first three requests on page two of the letter flow from Islamic strictures concerning modesty and mixing of the sexes. The fourth request asks for excusal from holiday

---

[3]Muslims recognize a continuous line of prophethood, beginning with Adam and extending through Noah (Nuh), Abraham (Ibrahim), Moses (Musa), and Jesus (Issa), among others. Islam teaches that Muhammad was the last prophet, who completed God's message to mankind. Muslims honor the Prophet Muhammad by using the expression "peace be upon him" after saying or writing his name. The Sunna or customary practice of the Prophet as reported by his Companions is a source of authority in Islam second only to the Qur'an.

activities that have "religious and social connotations contrary to Islamic faith and teachings."

The second set of requests, listed under "B" on pages two and three of the letter, touch on a number of other important Muslim beliefs and practices. To properly understand these requests, the reader needs to know more about the religious practices required of all Muslims.

The Five Pillars of Islam

Islam means submission to Allah (God), and a Muslim is one who submits to the will of Allah. The "Five Pillars of Islam" are:

1. Acceptance and repetition of the creed: "There is no God but Allah, and Muhammad is the prophet of Allah." This confession of faith and its faithful repetition constitute the first step in being a Muslim. The concept of unity (tawheed) stated in the creed has broad implications in the Islamic model for spiritual and social life.

2. Prayer: Every pious Muslim sets aside time each day for five acts of devotion and prayer. The first comes at dawn, the second at midday, the others at mid-afternoon, sunset, and after the fall of darkness or at bedtime.

Friday is the special day of community prayer. The faithful assemble in the mosque (masjid), the "place of prostration," for prayers. The service consists of a sermon from the imam followed by prayer.

3. Almsgiving: Muslims who have the means to do so are required to give to those who are less fortunate. Almsgiving is considered an act of worship because it is a form of offering thanks to Allah for the means of material well-being one has acquired.

4. Fasting during the sacred month of Ramadan[4]: During Ramadan all Muslims (except those in ill health) are required to abstain from food, drink, and sexual activity from dawn to sunset. The first day of the next month (Shawwal), is Eid Al-Fitr, "the festival of breaking off the fast." This festival is a joyous celebration, lasting in some places for three days.

5. Pilgrimage: Every Muslim hopes to be able to make the pilgrimage (Hajj) to the holy city of Mecca, in Saudi Arabia, at least once in a lifetime. Pilgrimage season begins in the tenth month, Shawwal, and

---

[4]Islamic years are reckoned on a lunar calendar of about 345 days divided into 12 months of 29 or 30 days. Ramadan is the ninth month. Islamic festivals occur 11 days earlier each year in relation to the solar calendar. Thus, in each 33-year cycle, the Ramadan fast will be observed in all seasons.

lasts through the middle of the twelfth month, Dhu al-Hijja. The rites and prayers of the pilgrimage take place at the sacred Ka'ba in Mecca and at other locations nearby.

The Ka'ba, focal point of prayer and destination of the pilgrimage, is the most important shrine in Islam. It is a cube-shaped, stone building in the center of the Great Mosque in Mecca. Embedded in its southeast corner is the Black Stone, believed by Muslims to have come from heaven in the days of Adam. Muslims associate the origin of the Hajj and the building of the Ka'ba with Abraham. Muslims venerate the Ka'ba as a symbol of unity and continuity of faith. Neither the Ka'ba nor the Black Stone are objects of worship. The principle of tawheed, or oneness of God, states that only He is worthy of worship.

On the tenth of Dhu al-Hijja, Muslims celebrate Eid Al-Adha, festival of the sacrifice. Although Muslims observe this holiday throughout the world, its most sacred observance is to be among the pilgrims at Mecca. The festival lasts for three days and marks the pilgrims' return to normal life.

There are other religious practices required by Islamic law in addition to the injunctions outlined in the Five Pillars. On page three of its letter, the ISNA alerts the public schools to the fact that Muslims must abstain from alcohol and avoid pig products in any form. Certain standards of cleanliness are also important, as indicated by the request for a water pipe in toilets.

The Religious Needs of Students and the First Amendment

All of the requests made in the letter express very real religious needs of a practicing Muslim attending public school. Some of the requests, however, call for accommodations that the schools, as state-sponsored institutions, may find difficult to make. At issue is a basic question that runs through the history of public education: To what extent may the state accommodate the needs and requirements of the religious communities represented in the schools? Or, to put it in a broader context, when does the No Establishment Clause of the First Amendment prohibit the state from accommodating the Free Exercise claims of religious groups?

The requirements of religious belief protected under the Free Exercise Clause of the First Amendment can come into tension with the No Establishment Clause when the practice of one's belief is conducted in a state institution such as a public school. The requirement not to hinder belief must be balanced by a sensitivity not to provide inadvertent state support for a particular belief. As we saw in the discussion of the school prayer controversy, some argue that state support is valid as long as it is nonpreferential, while others argue that no state support is allowable.

Many of the requests in the Islamic Society's letter may be easily granted by sensitive and thoughtful public school administrators without raising constitutional questions. Surely Muslim students should be able to wear modest clothing or refrain from attending social activities without violating school policies.

Students in most public schools are routinely allowed excused absences for religious holidays. Such a policy is generally considered to be a reasonable accommodation to the religious needs of a religiously diverse school population.

Some schools have excusal policies that allow students to opt out of limited portions of the curriculum that offend their religious beliefs. The easiest requests to grant are those focused on activities connected with such holidays as Halloween or Valentine's Day. If such requests cover significant academic portions of the curriculum, schools may be reluctant to excuse students on educational grounds. The ISNA request is a limited one, dealing with events and activities that sometimes accompany holidays in the schools. Most school officials will have little problem granting it.

Physical education, however, presents a number of difficulties, especially in school districts that now require coeducational PE classes. Here the public school's interest in developing a particular physical education curriculum may come into conflict with the religious practices of Muslims and others.

Is the public school that has coeducational physical education required to accommodate those groups who require separate classes for men and women? What about "only male/female instructors for the respective group"? In a recent case involving the Hasidic Jewish community in New York, the court ruled that the school was prohibited from putting up dividers separating men from women in the classroom. The school was also not required to provide separate bus drivers for male and female students. The results of this case would seem to suggest that the courts may not require public schools to create separate physical education classes for men and women.

One solution, of course, is to allow students to opt out of gym classes that would force them to violate their religious beliefs. Excusals of this kind would appear easy to grant without violating the First Amendment or seriously damaging the educational program of the school. Students could then be assigned to classes that are acceptable. But if acceptable classes are not available, is the school then required to arrange "alternate meaningful educational activities" for those students? One reading of the First Amendment might be that the state is *not required* to set up such classes, but *may do so* without violating the No Establishment Clause.

More difficult still is the question of whether or not the state should construct "separate and covered shower facilities for each student" or provide properly covered toilets with water pipes (the pipes provide water that is used as an alternative to toilet paper). Since such accommodations would involve spending tax money to meet the needs of a particular religious group, some will argue that the public schools are prohibited by the No Establishment Clause from making these changes. Others might appeal to the Free Exercise Clause, claiming that by not providing these facilities the state is forcing Muslims to choose between public education and obedience to the strictures of their faith. Here again, a third position might be that the schools are not required to provide such facilities, but may do so without "establishing" religion, especially if schools provide a secular reason for doing so that benefits many students. For schools with large Muslim populations, this last position may prove the only practical alternative.

The ISNA requests concerning labeling and preparation of food may also raise First Amendment, as well as practical, questions for some school officials. Schools, especially those with few Muslim students, may resist investing the time and money required to make these accommodations. And it is unlikely that the courts will compel school cafeterias to take into account the religious requirements of all students. Nevertheless, some schools do label food and provide a variety of selections in an effort to accommodate the health, dietary, and, in some cases, religious needs of their students.

Two requests concern the obligation to pray. Excusal for Friday prayer off-campus may present some practical problems for class scheduling, but there should be no legal barrier if it is construed as a "released time" program. In *Zorach v. Clausen* (1952), the Supreme Court ruled that schools may release students during school hours to participate in off-campus religious programs.

Schools may find it more difficult to excuse students "for 15 minutes in the afternoon to offer a special prayer in a designated area on the Campus." Since the time for prayer is somewhat flexible (mid-afternoon), schools may expect students to find time in their schedule to pray without interrupting class time (this may only be possible, of course, on the high school level). Public schools will certainly be challenged on constitutional grounds if a particular area of the school is designated as a place for prayer. The most an administrator may be able to do is to indicate what rooms, if any, are available to students for study or other activities between classes.

As reflection shows, these questions are challenging but not insuperable—especially if practical and constitutional solutions are sought in the light of the promise of American pluralism and the principles that lie behind our system of religious liberty.

Suggestions for Using the Document

Discussion Activities

1. After presenting background information about Islam, divide the class into groups. Each group is a committee appointed by the superintendent of schools to recommend a response to the letter from the Islamic Society of North America. Give each group a week to draft the response. Which requests can be accommodated? Which requests cannot be granted? Responses must be supported by practical and constitutional arguments.

   Share the letters in class. Compare the responses. Can the class reach a consensus on the major issues?

2. Assign a group of students to represent administrators. Without showing them the ISNA letter, give them a week to research the policies of the school and the school district concerning special requests from religious groups. Assign another group to represent Muslim parents. Ask them to research the tenets of Islam mentioned in the letter. Have the two groups role-play in class a meeting between the administrators and the parents.

3. After students have debated the issues raised by the letter, invite a local Muslim leader, an attorney familiar with school law, or both to meet with the class.

4. Ask the class to identify any school practices that already accommodate special requests unrelated to religion (e.g., excusal and absentee policies, need for special facilities). Discuss the differences, if any, between these requests and those based on religious belief.

5. Have the class examine existing school policies and practices. Do these policies and practices favor some religious groups over others or are they neutral toward religion in general?

Research Topics

1. Explore the history of Islam in the United States. When did the first Muslims come to America? Why is the Muslim population growing rapidly in the United States today?

2. How have special requests of other religious groups, such as Jehovah's Witnesses and the Amish, been treated by the public schools?

3.   What were the objections of many Roman Catholics and Jews to the public schools in the second half of the 19th century? How did the schools respond to those objections?

Additional Resources

Two films that focus on the challenges and opportunities of pluralism are:

Free to Be? New York City: Anti-Defamation League, distributor. Asks the viewer to think about questions raised by diversity and conformity in American life: What are the values of ethnic and religious group loyalty and identification, and what degree of assimilation is desirable in order to foster a united nation?

Religious Diversity. New York: Phoenix Films. Points out that religious liberty has allowed religions to flourish in the United States. Young people from a number of major faiths describe how they understand their religious beliefs and practices.

For publications about Islam and Muslims in America, contact:

The Islamic Society of North America
P.O. Box 36
Plainfield, Indiana 46168
The Middle East Institute
1761 N St. NW
Washington, D.C. 20036

PART
III

The Role of
Religion in the
Public School
Curriculum

Religion in the Public School Curriculum

Questions and Answers

Growing numbers of people in the United States think it is important to teach *about* religion in the public schools.[1] But what is the appropriate place of religion in the public school curriculum? How do we approach such issues as textbook content, values education, creation science, and religious holidays?

The following questions and answers are designed to assist school boards as they make decisions about the curriculum and educators as they teach about religion in ways that are constitutionally permissible, educationally sound, and sensitive to the beliefs of students and parents.

There are other questions concerning religion and the schools not addressed here, including school prayer, equal access, and how schools accommodate diverse religious beliefs and practices. For a full discussion of these broader issues, please contact the sponsors listed on pages 166–167.

Is it constitutional to teach about religion in public schools?

Yes. In the 1960s school prayer cases (which ruled against state-sponsored school prayer and Bible reading), the U.S. Supreme Court indicated that public school education may include teaching about religion. In *Abington v. Schempp* (1963), Associate Justice Tom Clark wrote for the Court:

> [I]t might well be said that one's education is not complete without a study of comparative religion or the history of religion and its relationship to the advancement of civilization. It certainly may be said that the Bible is worthy of study for its literary and historic qualities. Nothing we have said here indicates that such study of the Bible or of religion, when presented objectively as part of a secular program of education, may not be effected consistently with the First Amendment.

---

[1]Teaching about religion includes consideration of the beliefs and practices of religions; the role of religion in history and contemporary society; and religious themes in music, art, and literature.

What is meant by "teaching about religion" in the public schools?

The following statements distinguish between teaching about religion in public schools and religious indoctrination:

- The school's approach to religion is *academic*, not *devotional*.
- The school strives for student *awareness* of religions, but does not press for student *acceptance* of any one religion.
- The school sponsors *study* about religion, not the practice of religion.
- The school *exposes* students to a diversity of religious views; it does not *impose* any particular view.
- The school educates about all religions; it does not *promote* or *denigrate* any religion.
- The school *informs* students about various beliefs; it does not seek to *conform* students to any particular belief.[2]

Why should study about religion be included in the public school curriculum?

Because religion plays a significant role in history and society, study about religion is essential to understanding both our nation and the world. Omission of facts about religion can give students the false impression that the religious life of humankind is insignificant or unimportant. Failure to understand even the basic symbols, practices, and concepts of the various religions makes much of history, literature, art, and contemporary life unintelligible.

Study about religion is also important if students are to value religious liberty, the first freedom guaranteed in the Bill of Rights. Moreover, knowledge of the past and present roles of religion promotes the cross-cultural understanding that is essential to democracy and world peace.

Where does study about religion belong in the curriculum?

Wherever it naturally arises. On the secondary level, social studies, literature, and the arts offer many opportunities to include religious ideas and themes. On the elementary level, opportunities arise naturally in discussions of family and community life and in instruction about festivals and different cultures. Many educators believe that integrating study about religion into existing courses is an educa-

---

[2]This answer is based on guidelines originally published by the Public Education Religion Studies Center at Wright State University, Dayton, Ohio.

tionally sound way to acquaint students with the role of religion in history and society.

Religion also may be taught about in special courses or units. Some secondary schools, for example, offer such courses as world religions, the Bible as literature, and the religious literature of the West and of the East.

Do current textbooks teach about religion?

Rarely. Recent textbook studies conclude that most widely used textbooks largely ignore the role of religion in history and society. For example, readers of secondary U.S. history texts learn little or nothing about the great colonial revivals, the struggles of minority faiths, the religious motivations of immigrants, the contributions of religious groups to many social movements, major episodes of religious intolerance, and many other significant events of history. Education that fails to give appropriate attention to religious influences and themes is incomplete and inadequate education.

How does teaching about religion relate to the teaching of values?

Teaching about religion is not the same as teaching values. The former is objective, academic study; the latter involves the teaching of particular ethical viewpoints or standards of behavior.

There are basic moral values that are recognized by the population at large (for example, honesty, integrity, justice, compassion). These values can be taught in classes through discussion, by example, and by carrying out school policies. Teachers may not, however, invoke religious authority.

Public schools may teach about the various religious and non-religious perspectives concerning the many complex moral issues confronting society, but such perspectives must be presented without adopting, sponsoring, or denigrating any one view.

Is it constitutional to teach the biblical account of creation in the public schools?

Some states have passed laws requiring that creationist theory based on the biblical account be taught in the science classroom. The courts have found these laws to be unconstitutional on the grounds that they promote a particular religious view. The Supreme Court has acknowledged, however, that a variety of scientific theories about origins can be appropriately taught in the science classroom. In *Edwards v. Aguillard* (1988), the Court states:

> [T]eaching a variety of scientific theories about the origins of humankind to schoolchildren might be validly done with the clear secular intent of enhancing the effectiveness of science instruction.

Though science instruction may not endorse or promote religious doctrine, the account of creation found in various scriptures may be discussed in a religious studies class or in any course that considers religious explanations for the origin of life.

How should religious holidays be treated in the classroom?
Carefully. Religious holidays offer excellent opportunities to teach about religions in the elementary and secondary classroom. Recognition of and information about such holidays should focus on the origin, history, and generally agreed-upon meaning of the observances. If the approach is objective, neither advancing nor inhibiting religion, it can foster among students understanding and mutual respect within and beyond the local community.

These questions and answers are sponsored jointly by the following organizations:

American Academy of Religion
  Department of Religion
501 Hall of Languages,
  Syracuse University
Syracuse, New York 13244
315/423-4019

American Association of School
  Administrators
101 N. Moore St.
Arlington, Virginia 22209
703/528-0700

American Federation of Teachers
555 New Jersey Ave., NW
Washington, D.C. 20001
202/879-4400

American Jewish Congress
15 E. 84th St.
New York, New York 10028
212/879-4500

Americans United Research
  Foundation
900 Silver Spring Ave.
Silver Spring, Maryland 20910
301/588-2282

Association for Supervision and
  Curriculum Development
1250 N. Pitt St.
Alexandria, Virginia 22314
703/549-9110

Baptist Joint Committee on
  Public Affairs
200 Maryland Ave., NE
Washington, D.C. 20002
202/544-4226

Christian Legal Society
P.O. Box 1492
Merrifield, Virginia 22116
703/642-1070

The Church of Jesus Christ
of Latter-day Saints
50 E. North Temple
Salt Lake City, Utah 84150
801/240-1000

National Association of Evangelicals
1023 15th St., NW
Suite 500
Washington, D.C. 20005
202/789-1011

National Council of Churches
of Christ in the U.S.A.
475 Riverside Dr.
New York, New York 10115
212/870-2200

National Council for the
Social Studies
3501 Newark St., NW
Washington, D.C. 20016
202/966-7840

National School Boards
Association
1680 Duke St.
Alexandria, Virginia 22314
703/838-6722

The Islamic Society of North America
P.O. Box 38
Plainfield, Indiana 46168
317/839-8157

National Conference of Christians
and Jews
71 Fifth Ave., Suite 1100
New York, New York 10003
212/206-0006

National Council on Religion
and Public Education
N 162 Lagomarcino Hall
Iowa State University
Ames, Iowa 50011
515/294-7003

National Education Association
1201 16th St., NW
Washington, D.C. 20036
202/833-4000

Including the Study about Religions in the Social Studies Curriculum

*A Position Statement and Guidelines
from the National Council for the Social Studies
Adopted November 1984*

Position Statement

The National Council for the Social Studies in its Statement on Essentials of the Social Studies declares that:

Students need a knowledge of the world at large and the world at hand, the world of individuals and the world of institutions, the world past, and the world present and future.[1]

Religions have influenced the behavior of both individuals and nations, and have inspired some of the world's most beautiful art, architecture, literature, and music. History, our own nation's religious pluralism, and contemporary world events are testimony that religion has been and continues to be an important cultural value. The NCSS Curriculum Guidelines state that "the social studies program should draw from currently valid knowledge representative of human experience, culture, and beliefs."[2] The study about religions, then, has "a rightful place in the public school curriculum because of the pervasive nature of religious beliefs, practices, institutions, and sensitivities."[3]

Knowledge about religions is not only a characteristic of an educated person, but is also absolutely necessary for understanding and living in a world of diversity. Knowledge of religious differences and the

---

[1]"Statement on Essentials of the Social Studies." (March 1981). *Social Education* 45,3, p. 163.

[2]"A Revision of the NCSS Social Studies Curriculum Guidelines." (April 1979). *Social Education* 43,4, p.268.

[3]Collie, William E., and Lee H. Smith. (January 1981). "Teaching About Religion in the Schools: The Continuing Challenge." *Social Education* 45,1, p. 16.

role of religion in the contemporary world can help promote understanding and alleviate prejudice. Since the purpose of the social studies is to provide students with a knowledge of the world that has been, the world that is, and the world of the future, studying about religions should be an essential part of the social studies curriculum. Omitting study about religions gives students the impression that religions have not been and are not now part of the human experience. Study about religions may be dealt with in special courses and units or wherever and whenever knowledge of the religious dimension of human history and culture is needed for a balanced and comprehensive understanding.

In its 1963 decision in the case of Abington v. Schempp, the United States Supreme court declared that study about religions in the nation's public schools is both legal and desirable. Justice Tom Clark writing the majority opinion stated:

> In addition, it might well be said that one's education is not complete without a study of comparative religions or the history of religion and its relationship to the advancement of civilization. It certainly may be said that the Bible is worthy of study for its literary and historical qualities. Nothing we have said here indicates that such study of the Bible or of religion, when presented objectively as part of a secular program of education, may not be effected consistent with the First Amendment.

Justice William Brennan in a concurring opinion wrote:

> The holding of the Court today plainly does not foreclose teaching about the Holy Scriptures or about the differences between religious sects in classes in literature or history. Indeed, whether or not the Bible is involved, it would be impossible to teach meaningfully many subjects in the social sciences or the humanities without some mention of religion.

If the public schools are to provide students with a comprehensive education in the social studies, academic study about religions should be a part of the curriculum.

Guidelines

1. Study about religions should strive for awareness and understanding of the diversity of religions, religious experiences, religious expressions, and the reasons for particular expressions of religious beliefs within a society or culture.

2. Study about religions should stress the influence of religions on history, culture, the arts, and contemporary issues.

3. Study about religions should permit and encourage a comprehensive and balanced examination of the entire spectrum of ideas and attitudes pertaining to religion as a component of human culture.

4. Study about religions should investigate a broad range, both geographic and chronological, of religious beliefs, practices, and values.

5. Study about religions should examine the religious dimension of human existence in its broader cultural context, including its relation to economic, political, and social institutions as well as its relation to the arts, language, and literature.

6. Study about religions should deal with the world's religions from the same perspective (i.e., beginnings, historical development, sacred writings, beliefs, practices, values, and impact on history, culture, contemporary issues, and the arts).

7. Study about religions should be objective.

8. Study about religions should be academic in nature, stressing student awareness and understanding, not acceptance and/or conformity.

9. Study about religions should emphasize the necessity and importance of tolerance, respect, and mutual understanding in a nation and world of diversity.

10. Study about religions should be descriptive, non-confessional, and conducted in an environment free of advocacy.

11. Study about religions should seek to develop and utilize the various skills, attitudes, and abilities that are essential to history and the social sciences (i.e., locating, classifying, interpreting data; keen observation; critical reading, listening, and thinking; questioning; and effective communication).

12. Study about religions should be academically responsible and pedagogically sound, utilizing accepted methods and materials of the social sciences, history and literature.

13. Study about religions should involve a range of materials that provide a balanced and fair treatment of the subject, and distinguish between confessional and historical fact.

14. Study about religions should be conducted by qualified and certified teachers selected for their academic knowledge, their sensitivity and empathy for differing religious points of view, and their understanding of the Supreme Court's decisions pertaining to religious practices and study about religions in the public schools.

Recommendations for Teaching about Religions

*American Association of School Administrators**

- The study of religions in public schools is permitted by the Constitution as long as the subject matter is presented objectively as part of a secular program of education.

- Teachers of religion courses should be sensitive to varying beliefs of their students.

- The First Amendment does not forbid all mention of religion in the public schools. It does prohibit the advancement or inhibition of religion.

- Public Schools are not required to delete from their curriculum materials that may offend any religious sensibility.

- The decision to include—or exclude—material from the curriculum must be based on secular, not religious reasons.

- The material must be presented objectively.

- Religion should be taught with the same care and discipline as other academic courses.

- Schools should be especially sensitive to the developmental differences between elementary and secondary school students. Subjects or teaching methods that may be appropriate for secondary students may not be appropriate for younger children.

---

*An excerpt from *Religion in the Public Schools* (Arlington, Va.: American Association of School Administrators, 1986).

Religion in the Curriculum

Association for Supervision and Curriculum Development*

Recommendations

Clearly, decisive action is needed to end the current curricular silence on religion. We have discussed reasons for this silence (many of them misguided), and we have discussed some of its effects (chief among them ignorance and distortion). Our recommendations for ending the silence . . . bear reiterating briefly here:

1. Local decision making on the role of religion in the curriculum should be exercised within the context of religious diversity at the local, state, national and international levels.

2. Religious professionals and other community leaders should contribute, along with educators, to discussions of the role of religion in the curriculum, but the results of these deliberations should not be allowed to be shaped by particular ideological views.

3. Educators at all levels should be committed to the concept of a pluralistic and democratic society that accepts diversity of religious belief and practice as the norm.

4. State departments of education should address the issue of fair and factual treatment of religion in the curriculum by all local education agencies.

5. Textbook selection committees at the state, district and local school levels should require such treatment of religion in all curricular materials. To aid these committees in their selections, education agencies and professional organizations like ASCD should conduct staff development sessions on religion in the curriculum and issue specific guidelines concerning the treatment of religion in the textbooks.

6. Publishers should revise textbooks and other instructional materials to provide adequate treatment of diverse religions and their roles in American and world culture and to include appropriate religious and moral themes in literary and art history anthologies.

7. A major research and development effort should be undertaken to develop new curricular materials and instructional designs for teach-

---

**An excerpt from *Religion in the Curriculum: A Report from the ASCD Panel on Religion in the Curriculum* (Alexandria, Va.: Association for Supervision and Curriculum Development, August 1987).*

ing about religion within the various subject areas. Scholars and educators should work together to identify specific ideas, events, people and literature to be considered for inclusion in the curriculum.

8. Teacher educators, both preservice and inservice, should ensure that teachers acquire not only the substantive knowledge required to teach about religion in society but also the attitudes and understanding necessary to treat the subject with sensitivity in the classroom.

9. Teachers, administrators and members of the public should be aware of the impact of court decisions on the curriculum and should recognize that teaching about religion is not unconstitutional.

10. Teachers and administrators should analyze both the hidden and the explicit curriculums regularly to ensure sensitive concern for teaching about religion in society and for the faiths of individual students.

11. Educators should study federal court decisions regarding opting-out before developing their own policies, which should be applied strictly on a case-by-case basis. The option should be limited to those cases in which the material or content of instruction can be shown to significantly or substantially assault an individual's religious beliefs.

12. Local educators and their national organizations, including ASCD, should explore ways to foster public support for the teaching of rigorous, intellectually demanding accounts of religion in society, particularly in American society.

13. ASCD and other national education groups should aid educators in their deliberations on this matter by providing clear and accurate information on relevant court decisions, on curriculum development, on state and local textbook adoption criteria and on policy issues affecting the role of religion in the curriculum (with representative policy statements).

These recommendations . . . in no way advocate the teaching of religious belief or the sponsorship of religious practice in the public schools. To do so would be to trample . . . "humanity's boldest and most successful experiment in religious freedom."[1] But to understand America's bold experiment—and to understand the driving force of many historical and cultural movements worldwide—requires an understanding of the role religion has played, and continues to play, in human civilization.[2]

---

[1]Haynes, Charles C. (1986). *Religious Freedom in America: A Teacher's Guide.* Silver Spring, Md.: Americans United Research Foundation.

[2]Mead, Sidney. (1963). *The Lively Experiment.* New York: Harper and Row.

49 Ac